D0759863

WITHDRAWN

Louis Farrakhan
and the
Nation of Islam

Louis Farrakhan
and the
Nation of Islam

JIM HASKINS

Walker and Company
New York

First published in the United States of America in 1996
by Walker Publishing Company, Inc.

Published simultaneously in Canada by Thomas Allen & Son Canada,
Limited, Markham, Ontario

Library of Congress Cataloging-in-Publication Data
Haskins, James, 1941–
    Louis Farrakhan and the Nation of Islam / Jim Haskins.
        p.   cm.
    Includes bibliographical references and index.
    Summary: A biography of the Afro-American who dreamed of
a career as a violinist before joining the Nation of Islam and rising
in its ranks, eventually becoming its leader.
    ISBN 0-8027-8422-4.—ISBN 0-8027-8423-2 (reinforced)
    1. Farrakhan, Louis—Juvenile literature.   2. Black Muslims—
Biography—Juvenile literature.   [1. Farrakhan, Louis.   2. Black
Muslims.   3. Afro-Americans—Biography.]   I. Title.
BP223.Z8F384   1996
297'.87—dc20
[B]   96-3607
                                                                        CIP
                                                                         AC

Book design by Mary Jane DiMassi

Printed in the United States of America

2   4   6   8   10   9   7   5   3   1

To Pamela and Roger Webb

ACKNOWLEDGMENTS

I am grateful to Ann Kalkhoff, Katherine Trittschuh Morrison, and Mark Morrison for their help. A special thank-you to Kathy Benson.

Contents

1
Louis Farrakhan, Black Spokesman

Louis Farrakhan stood behind the bulletproof barrier on the steps of the Capitol Building in Washington, D.C., and looked out over an ocean of black faces. The crowd at the Million Man March on Monday, October 16, 1995, had far exceeded his hopes. Although the National Parks Service estimated the total number of people at 400,000, Farrakhan and other organizers of the march were certain they had exceeded their goal. And they had done so against every obstacle that could be put in their way. "Don't march," some of the most prominent black leaders had warned. "Louis Farrakhan is a hatemonger." The Anti-Defamation League, a Jewish group founded in 1913 to stop verbal attacks against Jewish people and to secure justice and fair treatment for all citizens alike, had taken out a full-page ad in major newspapers likening the march to a rally organized by the Ku Klux Klan. The media, in Farrakhan's view, had tried to exploit divisions in the black community to prevent black men from attending the march. But all attempts to sabotage the march had failed.

Louis Farrakhan, called a bigot, a hatemonger, a militant separatist, an anti-Semite, and a fringe group

Louis Farrakhan, guarded by members of the Fruit of Islam (FOI), at the Million Man March in Washington, D.C., October 16, 1995. (AP/Wide World Photos)

leader, felt vindicated. He looked out over the crowd and said, "I stand here today knowing . . . that my people have validated me. I don't need to be in any mainstream. I want to wash in the river of Jordan and the river that you see and the sea that is before us and behind us and around us. It's validation. That's the mainstream."[1]

Validation had been a long time coming for the sixty-two-year-old Farrakhan. As leader of the Nation of Islam, he could not claim a formal following of more than about 10,000 African-Americans—and that after twenty years as the organization's National Minister. But in recent years, he had found an eager audience among non-Muslim blacks as he articulated the bitterness they felt in a society in which racism seemed to run so deep it could never be uprooted. As America seemed to turn its back on the lofty ideals of equal opportunity it had embraced thirty years earlier during the civil rights movement, the mainstream black leadership seemed unable to respond effectively. The vacuum in black leadership had been practically an invitation to Louis Farrakhan, and he was smart enough to step in to fill the void.

In 1994, in an interview with Barbara Walters for the television news program "20/20," Louis Farrakhan referred to the indignities that black children must suffer even now. The transcript of the interview reads: "But the [ugly?] image is there. When I've got to go to school and read a textbook about Little Black Sambo. . . . When I've got to hear people calling me a burr-headed nigger and making a mockery of the thickness of my lips and the broadness of my nose. . . ."[2] Louis Farrakhan grew up in Boston in the 1940s; although he might not have had the exact experiences of which he spoke to Barbara Walters, he might well have. He knows that, even as a man over the age of sixty, he is still mocked by some whites simply because he is black. He also knows that he is feared by many whites simply because he is black—even by whites who might see a rare picture of him alone, not surrounded by bodyguards, and not recognize him as Minister Louis Farrakhan, leader of the Nation of Islam. He knows that, as a black man in America, he carries so much invisible baggage that a man with weaker convictions might stagger under the burden.

Louis Farrakhan is light-complected, and thus in his life he has had an easier time being accepted by whites, and often by his own people, than have his darker brothers. The bias against dark skin in American society has been so strong that it has even permeated the thinking of African-Americans. This color-consciousness is less strong now than it was in the past, but the fact remains that whites tend to favor lighter-complected blacks, and so they have traditionally had more opportunities. Aware of this fact, blacks have regarded the lighter-complected among them as somehow better, or at least potentially more successful.

After completing two years of teachers' college, Farrakhan might have gained a foothold on the ladder of success that is denied to poorly educated blacks. But Louis Farrakhan came to the conclusion in his early twenties that there was no real place for him in white society and that it was useless for him to hope that whites would ever accept him as a man and as an equal. He joined the Nation of Islam, an anti-white, separatist group, rose in its ranks, and eventually became its leader. The Nation of Islam is, and has always been, both a religion and an organization. Its membership is difficult to assess, because it is secretive and has never revealed its numbers or its inner workings. It is safe to say, however, that its formal membership is much smaller than the number of black people who describe themselves as followers of Louis Farrakhan.

Most black leaders, today and in the past, have tried

to appeal to the best instincts of whites, seeking justice and equality through the courts, through the taking of moral stands, through compromise instead of threats. But some black leaders have taken the opposite method, lashing out at white society, criticizing other black leaders who seek accommodation with whites, urging black separatism, speaking for the disaffected African-Americans who have no hope for a better future. Louis Farrakhan does both. On nationally televised programs such as "20/20" and "Donahue," he is charming and soft-spoken and nonthreatening in manner, although what he says may give his audiences pause. Listening to him, audiences wonder how he acquired a reputation as a firebrand. Like a patient teacher, he tells white questioners that they are miseducated and ignorant, through no fault of their own, of the history of slavery and the contributions of black people in history. Calmly and serenely, he tells white America that black people deserve a territory of their own, that black people have been exploited throughout their history, that black people are the original people of the earth. But with blacks, his manner changes.

When he speaks at a Nation of Islam mosque, or in a large urban auditorium to a huge, mostly black audience, he screams epithets against whites, charges that the evils African-Americans suffer, from unemployment, to drug addiction, to AIDs, are the results of white conspiracies, and warns that time is running out for America. Louis Farrakhan speaks to alienated black people who are sick and tired of the racism of the larger society and who despair of ever having an equal chance at education, housing, jobs, and opportunities for them-

**When he speaks to black audiences, Farrakhan screams epi-
thets against whites and charges that the evils that African-
Americans suffer, from unemployment to drug addiction to
AIDS, are the result of conspiracies by whites.** (AP/Wide World
Photos)

selves and their children. While his organization, the
Nation of Islam, is a fringe group in American society,
Louis Farrakhan is no fringe leader.

Since 1984, Louis Farrakhan has drawn especially
large audiences. That was the year the Reverend Jesse
Jackson made his first bid to become the Democratic
presidential candidate and Farrakhan supported him.
After Milton Coleman, a black reporter from the *Washington Post,* reported off-the-record remarks Jackson
made about Jews, Farrakhan apparently threatened
Coleman's life and characterized Judaism as a "gutter

religion." The episode dashed whatever slim hopes Jackson had for making a respectable showing in the primary elections. It also put Minister Louis Farrakhan in the national spotlight. He has rarely been out of it since.

There are some who feel that without that media spotlight Louis Farrakhan would have little influence on African-Americans. Although to many people it seems that Farrakhan harbors a special paranoia about and hatred toward Jews that stands out sharply from his more rational anger at white society in general, others feel that Farrakhan's criticisms—or those of his lieutenants—of the Jewish religion and Jewish people have been calculated attempts to keep him in the spotlight. But if the Jackson campaign scandal elevated him to a position as a militant black spokesman, it is not just anti-Semitic statements that have kept Louis Farrakhan in the spotlight. His strong statements against white America strike a chord deep within African-Americans—even within those who disagree with most of what he stands for. He puts into words what they cannot; he acts on their behalf. As such, he continues a long line of militant, outspoken blacks who have taken, or attempted to take, leadership positions in African America. What distinguishes Louis Farrakhan is how prominent he has become; no other militant black leader in American history has achieved such prominence.

2
The Latest of a Line

In all the years African-Americans have lived in the
United States, they have resisted the conditions of slavery and servitude and second-class citizenship that have
been forced upon them by the majority white culture.
Some have sought acceptance by and integration into
that majority culture; others have decided that to seek
acceptance is useless and have sought either the violent
overthrow of the society or separation from it. Black
militant and separatist feeling goes back to slave revolts
in colonial times, a substantial number of them led by
slave preachers—including one in 1816 in South Carolina and Nat Turner's rebellion in Southampton, Virginia, in 1831.

By the early years of the new nation, some blacks
had concluded that there was simply no place for them
in the United States. Paul Cuffe, a successful Massachusetts ship owner, was so incensed by slavery and by the
failure of the new nation to keep its revolutionary promise of equality that he decided the best course for free
blacks was to return to Africa. He had his sights set on
the country of Sierra Leone in Africa and actually made

several trips there; but he died before he could realize his dream.

A similar dream propelled those blacks who signed up with the American Colonization Society, founded by whites around the time of Cuffe's death and sponsored by, among others, President James Monroe. Its purpose was to establish an African homeland for freed slaves. In 1821, the organization bought land in Africa and built the settlement of Monrovia, which later became the capital of the colony of Liberia. By 1860, more than 11,000 blacks had been sent to Monrovia, although some eventually returned. The Civil War and the Emancipation Proclamation brought an end to the active period of the American Colonization Society.

Beginning in the 1830s, many blacks, especially escaped slaves, made their way to Canada, where they settled and began new lives. But the migration of blacks to Canada slowed considerably after the Civil War and Emancipation.

Not long after the end of the Civil War, some former slaves realized that the promise of the Emancipation Proclamation was little more than empty words. Although blacks were able to go to school, vote, and even hold office in new southern state governments, there was little real effort to establish them on an equal footing with whites. The Freedmen's Bureau, established by the federal government, tried to help former slaves adjust to their new lives, but most of the former slaves were uneducated and unskilled except in agriculture. Without land and farm animals and equipment, they had no hope of establishing free and independent lives. Most remained with, or returned to, their former masters and settled into the semi-slavery of sharecropping. A black man named Benjamin "Pap" Singleton was convinced that true freedom would never be had in the old South and that the only course for former slaves was to create a free and independent black nation in the United States. In late 1879, Singleton led some 7,500 blacks, most of them former slaves, from Alabama, Georgia, Mississippi, and Texas to Kansas, where he planned to create a black nation state. But after a short time, about three-quarters of the people returned to the South because they were unable to make it on the prairie frontier.

Some thirty years later, another leader arose who believed that African-Americans could never live free in the United States. During World War I, a Jamaican named Marcus Garvey arrived in New York preaching

Marcus Garvey, a Jamaican immigrant, built a large following with his black nationalist message during World War I. Garvey's United Negro Improvement Association (UNIA) had a very complex hierarchy of officials; its members wore special uniforms on ceremonial occasions.
(AP/Wide World Photos)

black nationalism. He established an organization called the Universal Negro Improvement Association (UNIA), which had a newspaper, regular meetings, and a very complex hierarchy of officials. Members of the UNIA wore uniforms and held large parades and other public demonstrations, and attracted a considerable following. Having built a following, Garvey started several businesses, most notably the Black Star Line of ships. He also started a Back to Africa movement, because he was convinced that the black man would never enjoy equal rights in America. He was supported in this movement by the Ku Klux Klan, whose leaders he met, for he had much in common with white racists who wished America free of nonwhites, among others (the Klan was also against Catholics and Jews).

Unfortunately for Garvey and his followers, the United States government indicted him on charges of mail fraud; Garvey was convicted and deported back to Jamaica. He was unable to continue his movement, and those he left behind were unable to go on without his leadership.

The next black separatist movement started in Detroit in the early 1930s. The Nation of Islam had its beginnings there, under the inspiration of a mysterious man named W. D. Fard, who purported to bring the world religion of Islam to African-Americans. His staunchest convert was a man named Elijah Poole, who later took the name Elijah Muhammad. After Fard disappeared mysteriously, Muhammad built the membership of the Nation of Islam by attracting imprisoned men to the rigid discipline and message of hope of the Nation. It was Muhammad's dream for the Nation to be self-supporting, and under his leadership the Nation started a variety of business enterprises.

Muhammad's most famous follower, Malcolm X, converted to the Nation while in prison. The charismatic Malcolm X attracted many more members with his railings against "white devils." His calls for a separate nation put the Nation of Islam on the map. Nation of Islam temples were established in dozens of cities; and as Elijah Muhammad's National Minister, Malcolm X brought unprecedented media attention to the Nation. But Malcolm X later split with Elijah Muhammad and was assassinated by followers of Muhammad in 1965 before he could establish a new organization. The defection of Malcolm X caused the Nation to lose credibility and membership; and after Elijah Muhammad died and his son, W. D. Muhammad, tried to move the organization closer to the world religion of Islam, Louis Farrakhan tried to reinvigorate the old Nation of Islam without much success.

Stokely Carmichael tried to step into the militant black leadership void with his call for "Black Power!" Carmichael and his followers had gained control of the interracial, nonviolent civil rights organization known as the Student Nonviolent Coordinating Committee (SNCC), after its members had suffered brutal beatings, arrests, and killings at the hands of white racists when it tried to conduct a voter registration drive in Alabama in the summer of 1964. Whites had been expelled from the organization, and the N word in its name had been changed from Nonviolent to National. But "Black Power!" turned out to be more words than program.

After the assassination of Malcolm X in 1965, Stokely Carmichael of the Student Nonviolent Coordinating Committee (SNCC) tried to step into the militant black leadership void with his call for "Black Power!" in 1966. (AP/Wide World Photos)

In 1966, the same year Stokely Carmichael called for "Black Power!" the Black Panther Party was formed in Oakland, California. Its leaders immediately grabbed the attention of the country by appearing at the state capitol in Sacramento carrying rifles. The Black Panthers preached militant self-defense, demanded federal money for programs for the black community, and sought to make alliances with both black and white radical groups for the purpose of overthrowing the system. Among these alliances was one with SNCC, under the leadership of Stokely Carmichael. Panther leaders such as Huey Newton and Eldridge Cleaver, a former convict

The Black Panther Party for Self-Defense was formed in Oakland, California, in 1966. Its founders, Bobby Seale, left, and Huey P. Newton, carried weapons openly and announced that they would protect black ghetto neighborhoods from racist police. (AP/Wide World Photos)

like Malcolm X, attracted many disaffected black youth with their attitude of pride and reckless determination to defend themselves and their communities. But the Panthers were soon at war not only with local police but also with other militant black organizations. Within a few years, most of its membership had been either arrested and imprisoned, killed in shoot-outs, or forced into exile abroad.

There followed a void in black militant leadership on a national level until Jesse Jackson's 1984 presidential campaign, when Louis Farrakhan stepped into the breach. At the time there was a lot of pent-up resentment among black people—not just among those trapped in urban ghettos but those who had made it into the middle class. The ghetto dwellers saw little improvement in their lives from the time of segregation. Those who had managed to take advantage of the gains made by the civil rights movement still faced daily affronts to their dignity, whether it was the subtle movement of a white person away from them on a bus, or the obvious lie of a white landlord saying the apartment advertised for rental was no longer available, or the suspicion that too many stories in the media about crime and drugs were illustrated by black faces. It made them feel good to know that Louis Farrakhan was telling "whitey" off. In some ways, it didn't matter who was doing that telling; it could have been anybody. But in other ways, it could only have been Louis Farrakhan at this moment in the history of race relations.

3
The Early Life of Louis Farrakhan

A common phrase that is often repeated among members of the Nation of Islam is "Those who know don't say and those who say don't know." The Nation is, and always has been, secretive about its inner workings. The same is true of its leader, Louis Abdul Farrakhan. In interviews, he deflects questions about his personal life just as he demurs when asked to give an estimate of the membership of the Nation of Islam. Only the sketchiest information is known, and thus it is difficult to try to understand the man and his motivations.

He was born Louis Eugene Walcott on May 11, 1933, in the borough of the Bronx in New York City. His mother, who worked as a domestic, was from Baltimore, Maryland, and his father, described in some sources as a domestic as well and in others as a schoolteacher and Baptist preacher, had immigrated from Jamaica.

Louis hardly knew his father, who died when he was only three. The loss must have affected him deeply, and the need for a father figure may have been one reason why he was so deeply influenced by the strong male culture of the Nation of Islam, and by the strong men who were its leaders in the mid-1950s—Malcolm X and Elijah Muhammad.

After his father's death, Louis and his mother moved to Roxbury, a predominantly black section of Boston, Massachusetts, probably to be closer to other relatives. The economic struggles the family experienced with only his mother's wages to rely on must have affected him, too.

When Louis was born, the United States was deeply segregated. Life was difficult even for African-Americans in two-parent households with steady incomes; it was doubly difficult for a widowed domestic worker with a child. Although legal segregation existed only in the South, segregation was also the custom in the northern states. More than most blacks, domestic workers were forced to experience daily the insults and slights of prejudice. Young Louis Walcott must have resented the white families for whom his mother worked—for taking her away from him, for not treating her with respect, for having life so much easier simply because of the color of their skin.

Louis's mother worked hard to care for her son and to raise him to be a good man with ambition and character. Years later, Farrakhan recalled that she instilled in him a love of and a pride in being black: "She made me to know my history, to know my roots, so I grew up with a love for myself and secure within myself, never feeling inferior and certainly not feeling superior."[1]

His mother considered religion and churchgoing very important, and Louis was brought up in the St. Cyprian Episcopal Church on Tremont Street, where he was a choirboy. In addition to honing his musical skills, serving in the church junior choir helped Louis practice his diction. He had a stuttering problem when he spoke, but the stutter left him when he sang.

Despite the good things a strict religious upbringing did for him, Louis would later look back on the teachings of Christianity as harmful to him as a black person, for in Christian belief black skin was a curse because blacks were descended from Ham. According to the story in the Bible, Ham was one of the sons of Noah. Ham got drunk and mocked Noah, causing Noah to put a curse on him and to doom him to be a hewer of wood and a drawer of water.

Moreover, the images of people in the Christianity in which Louis Walcott was raised were of white people—from Jesus Christ to Mary to John the Baptist. Because of these Christian teachings, it must have been difficult for a young boy with darker skin to feel proud of who he was, despite all the best efforts of his mother.

Louis was an excellent student in the mostly black elementary and junior high schools he attended and was accepted at the prestigious Boston English High School, whose student body was mostly white. Rather than crawling into a shell, the bespectacled, shy, soft-spoken student was determined to prove he could excel—at everything. He conquered his stutter, and became not only an honor student but also a talented actor and a skilled athlete. Track was his best sport, and he was a member of the 1950 state championship track team. But his special skill was in music, particularly on the violin, which he played in the school orchestra as well as at home. He regularly practiced three, four, and five

hours a day, usually in the bathroom, because, he once
explained, "the violin seemed to resonate better there."[2]

When he thought about his career plans, Louis
dreamed of being a violinist. In 1946, he was one of the
first blacks to appear on Ted Mack's television show,
"The Original Amateur Hour," then a popular TV ama-
teur-talent show. But his mother wanted him to go to
college and get a degree and become a teacher, one of
the professions to which blacks could aspire if they
sought a middle-class life. Dutifully, Louis enrolled at
Winston-Salem State Teachers College in North Carolina, which had offered him a scholarship in track.

When he departed for Winston-Salem, Louis left
behind not only his home, his mother, and his friends
but also his childhood sweetheart, Betsy Ross. The
young lovers found it difficult to be apart, and when, at
the end of Louis's junior year at college, Betsy became
pregnant with the first of their nine children, he
dropped out of college and returned to Boston. He and
Betsy were married in 1954.

That year, the United States Supreme Court ruled
in *Brown v. Board of Education*, a school desegregation
case. In its landmark decision, the Court declared "separate but equal" education unconstitutional and stated
that desegregation of schools in those areas where segregation was the law should proceed "with all deliberate
speed." Many blacks, and their white supporters, hailed
the decision as a major crack in the wall of segregation,
and looked forward to the end of such laws in other
areas of life as well. For Louis and Betsy Walcott, it was
a bright note on which to start their life together; both

hoped that life would be easier and filled with greater opportunities for them, and especially for their children. To support himself and his family, Louis became a professional musician. Although his first love was the classical violin, pursuing a career in that field would have required him to have additional schooling at a music conservatory. While at college he had taken up the guitar, and it was as a singer/guitar player that he set out to seek his fortune. Accompanying himself on that instrument, he sang both country music and calypso, the lilting music of his Caribbean heritage. He was billed sometimes as "Calypso Gene" and sometimes as "The Charmer."

Boston was a college town, with many clubs and coffeehouses that hired individual musicians, usually singer/guitarists. Calypso singing and music were enjoying a vogue, due in great measure to the popularity of another handsome performer named Harry Belafonte. Whether appearing as "Calypso Gene" or "The Charmer," Louis Walcott did well in his career and was soon playing in the better clubs in Boston and around the country.

While entertaining in the Boston area Louis Walcott first met Malcolm X, the minister of Boston's Muslim Temple No. 11. Malcolm X was a tall, light-complected man with reddish hair and glasses, whose erect and proud carriage made him stand out immediately. Additionally, he was a charismatic speaker who preached that blacks were God's chosen people, although Malcolm called God by the name Allah. Intrigued by the man and the message he carried, Louis began to pay attention to the small but growing Nation of Islam movement in Boston's black community. The men always wore suits and bow ties and were clean-shaven. The women covered their heads and wore long dresses. They led very disciplined lives and did not smoke or drink alcohol or eat pork. All the men had jobs. It was said that the majority of the men were former convicts, like Malcolm X. The change that had been wrought in them by the Nation of Islam was remarkable.

Then, in 1955, Louis Walcott had an experience that changed his life forever and provided him immediately with the greater opportunities he had envisioned, although not in the way he had expected. While performing in Chicago, he was invited to the Nation of Islam's annual Savior's Day service, which featured a speech by the Honorable Elijah Muhammad, who was at that time the Black Muslims' maximum leader. In Elijah Muhammad, Louis Walcott found the father he had lost as a young child. Almost immediately, he joined the Nation of Islam.

4

The Nation of Islam

By 1955, the Nation of Islam had existed for a quarter
of a century. When it was founded in Detroit, Michigan,
in 1930, the first year of the Great Depression, Detroit's
black neighborhoods were in the grip of fear and anxi-
ety. Between 1900 and 1930, a great migration of
African-Americans from the South had swelled the
black populations of Detroit and other northern cities.
The number of African-Americans in Detroit had
jumped an astonishing 600 percent just in the ten years
between 1910 and 1920. Crop failures, floods, infesta-
tions of boll weevils, and anti-black feeling in the South
had hastened the departure of these migrants, who at
first had been welcomed in the North—or at least their
labor had been welcomed. Especially during World War
I (1914–1917), more manpower was needed to run the
northern factories that produced everything from ships
to tires to steel, and wartime restrictions on immigration
had cut off the normal flow of European immigrants.

The new arrivals had crowded into existing black
neighborhoods until these areas had overflowed with
migrants, and then taken over adjoining areas as whites
moved out. Life was not easy, and northern blacks suf-

fered from discrimination in housing, education, and other areas of life. But there was much greater opportunity—and much less actual segregation—in the North than in the South. Even after the war was over, black northerners were able to continue making a living, as postwar prosperity kept the factories humming. But when the New York Stock Market crashed in the fall of 1929, wiping out scores of businesses, not to mention the savings of millions of Americans, blacks knew very well that their economic lives would be affected, too. Always "last hired," even in good times, they were "first fired" now, and they did not have the same avenues of recourse available to them as white workers had. All the labor unions in the United States were for whites only; it would be several years before black labor leader A. Philip Randolph succeeded in establishing the first black union, the Brotherhood of Sleeping Car Porters. The resentment of blacks against white America for treating them as second-class citizens grew, and some were ripe for the influence of people and movements that spoke against the American system.

Communism, instituted in Russia after the First World War, was a doctrine that preached against the holding of wealth by a small class of people and declared that all people were equal, no matter what their color. The American Communist Party targeted blacks and made great strides in recruiting black members after the International Labor Defense, a Communist legal organization, stepped forward to defend the Scottsboro Boys, nine young black men who were falsely accused of raping two white women in Alabama and quickly sentenced to die. But the membership of the American Communist Party was predominantly white, and many blacks were skeptical of its commitment to true equality.

Some blacks were far more willing to listen to a man variously known as Wallace D. Fard, Mr. Farrad Mohammad, Mr. F. Mohammad Ali, Professor Ford, and Mr. Wali Farrad. His racial and national identity was uncertain. He was thought by some to be an Arab, but some legends about him describe him as a black Jamaican whose father was a Syrian Moslem. A peddler by trade, he went from house to house carrying silks and telling potential buyers that the lush fabrics were from their home country. Naturally, that made people curious, and he would then explain that he was from the holy city of Mecca in Saudi Arabia and talk about what he called Afro-Asia. He was well-read and well-spoken, and he found a welcome in many black Detroit homes. One woman recalled what happened after he was invited to a dinner that included pork: "He would eat whatever we had on the table, but after the meal he began to talk. 'Now don't eat this food, it is poison for you. The people in your own country do not eat it. Since they eat the right kind of food they have the best health all the time. If you would just live like the people in your home country, you would never be sick anymore.' So we all wanted him to tell us about ourselves and about our home country and about how we could be free from rheumatism, aches, and pains."[1]

Eventually, Fard explained that his real mission in the United States was to awaken American blacks to "the truth about the white man, and to prepare [them] for the Armageddon."[2]

Most among Fard's first small audiences were churchgoing, Bible-reading Christians who understood what Armageddon was. Fard offered his interpretation: In the Book of Revelation it is promised that there will be a final battle between good and evil and that this decisive battle will take place in Har-Magedon, "the Mountain of Megiddo," in the Great Plain of Esdraelon in Asia Minor. Good and evil, Fard assured his listeners, were the forces of black and white; the Valley of Esdraelon actually symbolized North America; and the battle of Armageddon was the final confrontation of the black man with the race of people who have long oppressed him, whites.[3]

There were other ways in which religious blacks could appreciate Fard's message. He said that God's real name was Allah and that the faith he preached was based on Islam, a world faith. Islam had arisen in the Arab world in the late sixth century A.D. and was an outgrowth of both Judaism and Christianity. It owes its existence to one remarkable man, Muhammad, born around 560 A.D., who was reared in a belief system that worshiped many gods, although there was general agreement that high over them all stood a supreme god, creator and ruler of the world, who was called Allah.

Muhammad spent the first part of his life believing in those many gods, as well as in Allah. But he came into contact with many Arab-speaking Jewish and Christian people and learned that they believed in only one god. Muhammad began to have strange dreams and visions, and one day he had a life-changing vision in which he was visited by the angel Gabriel, who called him to be God's prophet. He was persuaded that there was only one God, Allah, and he began to carry the word to all who would listen to him. His primary message was that men must voluntarily surrender their lives to Allah. To designate this submission, Muhammad used the term *Islam*, and he who submitted was called a *Muslim*. By his own insistence, Muhammad was the first Muslim and God's final messenger, sent to warn the Arabs that they must come face-to-face with God with nothing between them—not other gods, priests, or ceremonies. He began to set down in writing the various revelations he received from Allah through the angel Gabriel. A few years after his death, these revelations and the recollections of his companions would be compiled in the form of the holy book of Islam, the Koran, or Qu'ran.

Muhammad attracted many converts during his lifetime, but it was after his death that his followers expanded Islam. In less than one hundred years, the Islamic world extended over Morocco, Spain, and France to the west, and to Constantinople, across central Asia, and up the Indus River to the east. Until the expansion of Christian missionary activity in the 1800s, Islam encompassed a wider variety of races than any other religion; by 1930 it was the main religion in a wide range of territory extending across North Africa and western Asia, eastward through central Asia in China, and then southward to Pakistan. Smaller groups of Muslims could be found in India, Malaya, the Philippines, Tanzania, the Balkan countries, southern Russia, and South America. It had as yet made few inroads into North America, and world Islam would not reach North America in any significant way until non-European immigration began in large numbers after World War II.

W. D. Fard's brand of Islam was very different from world Islam. For one thing, it focused on American blacks, which world Islam did not do. It proclaimed that American blacks constituted the Lost Found Nation of Islam, the descendants of the Asian Black Nation and of the tribe of Shabazz, which had come to earth when a great explosion had divided the earth and the moon sixty trillion years earlier. There were, in fact, no white people until an evil black scientist named Yakub, who rebelled against Allah, created them in his laboratory, grafting out all humanity from them. These devils had been given six thousand years to rule, an allotted span that had ended in 1914. The years since had been merely a "grace period" that would last no longer than it was necessary for the chosen of Allah to be resurrected from the mental death imposed upon them by the white man.

To many blacks in Detroit, Fard's brand of Islam was a revelation, particularly its anti-white message. He was not the first black man to preach anti-white sentiments. Some remembered Jamaican immigrant Marcus Garvey and his UNIA and Back to Africa movements. But Fard's message was different: American blacks were to stay right there in America and, eventually, claim it for themselves.

As Fard's message spread, people began holding meetings in their homes so he could speak to their friends and neighbors. When these meeting places became too small, they rented a hall, and there Fard established a Temple of Islam in Detroit.

With this first Temple of Islam, Fard had a home for his movement, and he wasted no time in establishing a tight organizational structure. Membership was formalized; Fard interviewed potential recruits and then registered them. He established a regular schedule of meetings and services and introduced various rituals to replace the familiar rituals of Christianity he had asked his followers to leave behind. He became more daring in his preaching, telling his followers that they were not Negroes but Black Men, and that they had been stolen away from their homeland and enslaved by evil white men. Their names, he told them, were slave names, to be cast off in favor of new, Muslim names. In fact, one of the steps in the initiation process into the Nation of Islam was to write a letter to Fard asking for his or her "original" name. Fard would then provide an Islamic surname, after which the new member would discard his or her "slave name."

Most daringly, he attacked the teachings of the Bible as a white man's book. This was daring because most of his followers had grown up as Christians and believing in the Bible. That is not to say that he rejected all of Christianity or did not teach from the Bible. He explained that Jesus Christ did exist and was a holy man, one of the three great prophets of Islam. But the white, blue-eyed Jesus of Christianity was not the real Jesus, who would someday be revealed as the brown-skinned man he truly was.

Fard often used the Bible as his text, but explained its stories and prophecies with an interpretation much different from any his followers had ever heard before. He also, of course, used the holy book of the religion of Islam, the Qu'ran or Koran, and wrote two manuals of his own, *The Secret Ritual of the Nation of Islam* and

Teaching for the Lost Found Nation of Islam in a Mathematical Way, which was written in his own "symbolic language" and could not be understood without his interpretation.

Once he had a temple, Fard set up a school, which he called the University of Islam and which was intended for the education of children in the movement. He arranged for interested new members who could not read to be tutored by volunteers so they could learn for themselves the truths that the white man had long denied them. Fard created a Muslim Girls Training Class to teach young women how to be proper wives, mothers, and homemakers. And finally, out of concern for potential trouble with nonbelievers or with the police, he created a military organization that he called the Fruit of Islam, for which men were trained in military tactics and the use of firearms.

Within three years, Fard had succeeded in establishing a well-organized and tightly run organization. He then proceeded to select and personally train a Minister of Islam and a group of assistant ministers to run it.

Among these first officers of the movement was Elijah Muhammad, born Elijah Poole in Georgia, whose family had migrated to Detroit in the 1920s. Several members of the Poole family were early converts to the Nation of Islam. In fact, Elijah and two of his brothers decided to seek membership together and wrote a letter to Fard asking him to give them their original names. In the letter they neglected to mention that they were blood brothers, and Fard was most likely unaccustomed to getting three converts from the same family at the same time. The original surnames he bestowed upon them were all different; but when it was pointed out to them that blood brothers might be expected to have the same surname, Fard explained that he had "divine knowledge" of the real names of the three brothers.

Elijah Poole's first "original" name given by Fard was Karriem. But he soon distinguished himself in Fard's eyes and was given the name Muhammad as a mark of higher status.

Disagreements and factionalism threatened the Nation of Islam almost from the first. W. D. Fard's willingness to have his Fruit of Islam take up arms disturbed some members, as did his teaching that his followers were not Americans and owed no loyalty to their country of birth. These teachings caused another trusted lieutenant, Abdul Muhammad, to break away from Fard's group and found his own organization, one that stressed complete loyalty to the American Constitution and flag. This group did not last long, however.

The American Communist Party, anxious to attract more black members, tried to infiltrate the Nation of Islam early on and to turn the organizational aspects already in place to their own purposes. Anti-union interests hoped to use the Nation against efforts to unionize blacks. There was even some international interest. One Ethiopian tried to involve the Muslims in investment deals to aid his nation. The Japanese, at the time hostile to the United States, attempted to gain a foothold in the Nation. Some members of the Nation did leave in favor of the Japanese, but this movement went nowhere.

In spite of these various efforts to split the group, under W. D. Fard it remained strong and continued to grow. Temple No. 2 was established in Chicago, and the beginnings of what would become Temple No. 3 was started in Milwaukee. By 1934 the Nation had a membership estimated at about 8,000. When it came time for Fard to name a Minister of Islam to take over the daily operations of the movement, he chose Elijah Muhammad.

As he handed off responsibility to others, Fard gradually withdrew from the public eye. Then, in 1934, he disappeared altogether. What happened to him is not known. There were rumors that he had returned to his native land. Some hinted that he had been done away with by the police or by dissident factions within his movement. Critics of Elijah Muhammad charged that he'd engineered Fard's disappearance so that he could take control of the Nation. In fact, Muhammad did take over leadership of the movement, but he had been chosen to do so by Fard, selected as the chief minister of the Nation before Fard's disappearance.

Without Fard, the movement lost its way for a time and began to decline in both membership and influence. Elijah Muhammad could not control the factions in the Detroit Temple No. 1. To escape the infighting, he went to Chicago, where he made his headquarters until more factionalism forced him to flee to Washington, D.C., where he began Temple No. 4. For the next several years, he moved from city to city, never staying too long in one place and being forced to visit his wife and eight children in secret.

In 1941, the United States entered World War II on both the European and Pacific fronts, and all able-bodied men were called to serve their country through military service. In 1942, Elijah Muhammad was arrested on charges of draft-dodging and sentenced to five years in prison. He later told Malcolm X that it was enemies in the black community who had engineered his arrest and conviction on the trumped-up charge, for he was too old to have served in the military. Released in 1946, after three and a half years, he returned to his work, managing to regain control of a Nation of Islam weakened by factionalism and to begin the process of remaking it as he thought it ought to be.

Central to Muhammad's plan was the elevation of Fard as a deity. Fard became closely associated with Allah and was believed to have been Allah on earth. As a close associate of Allah, Muhammad thus became the Prophet or Messenger of Allah. Elijah Muhammad's organizational abilities and sense of mission soon overcame the earlier factionalism. Detroit's Temple No. 1 came back into the fold, and membership and sense of purpose began to increase again.

Far more than a religion, the Nation of Islam was a way of life. Temple services and meetings were held several times a week. In addition to learning about the history of black people in the world and of how the white man had enslaved African-Americans and caused them to be "lost," Muslims were admonished to live clean, respectable lives. Like the faithful of world Islam, members of the Nation of Islam did not smoke or drink or eat pork. They had jobs and close family lives. Men and women were expected to follow strict rules governing relationships between them; husbands and wives each had duties to the family.

All members of the Nation of Islam were expected

Under the leadership of Elijah Muhammad, shown here at right at a Chicago rally in 1961, the Nation of Islam had remarkable success in converting prisoners. Easily the most famous prisoner-convert to the Nation was Malcolm X (center). (AP/Wide World Photos)

to attend the frequent meetings and services, to save their money, and to give a fixed percentage of their income to the Nation. By following the rules of the Nation, many formerly poor, illiterate, and hopeless black people became stable and prosperous. In 1938, a sociologist named Erdmann D. Beynon published in the

American Journal of Sociology an article titled "The Voodoo Cult Among Negro Migrants in Detroit." In the course of his study, he had noted the remarkable effect membership in the Nation, which he referred to as a cult, had had on some of these migrants. In the early 1930s he reported, "At the time of their first contact with the prophet, practically all of the members of the cult were recipients of public welfare, unemployed, and living in the most deteriorated areas of Negro settlement in Detroit. . . . At the present time, there is no known case of unemployment among these people. Practically all of them are working in the automobile and other factories. They live no longer in the slum section, but rent homes in some of the best economic areas in which Negroes have settled. They tend to purchase more expensive furniture, automobiles, and clothes than do their neighbors even in these areas of higher-class residence."[4]

Perhaps the most remarkable success the Nation of Islam enjoyed in membership recruitment was among black prisoners, and it was a prisoner named Malcolm Little whose recruitment would change the course of the Nation.

5
Malcolm X Joins the Nation of Islam

Malcolm X was born Malcolm Little in Omaha, Nebraska, on May 19, 1925. His father, the Reverend Earl Little, was a follower of Marcus Garvey and an energetic organizer for Garvey's United Negro Improvement Association. The Reverend Little's black nationalist activities were considered dangerous by most whites, and the family had to move several times because of threats to the Reverend Little's life. In Lansing, Michigan, in 1931, those threats were carried out. Malcolm was only six years old when his father was murdered. In all probability, he was attacked and then his body laid across the streetcar tracks to be run over. The killer or killers were never found.

Left with eight children and no way to support them, Malcolm's mother went on welfare. But the stress of her husband's death and the responsibility of the family caused her to become mentally unbalanced. The children were taken from her, and she was placed in a state mental institution.

Malcolm lived with a succession of foster families and spent time in a reform school. Then, just after he completed seventh grade, his half sister Ella Little, the

Reverend Little's daughter by an earlier marriage, arrived from Boston to visit the children. She invited Malcolm to spend the summer with her in Boston, and he found the city much more to his liking than any place in Michigan he had lived. Ella Little arranged with the juvenile authorities in Michigan to have Malcolm live with her, and he went to Boston for good after he finished eighth grade.

Ella Little had hoped to influence Malcolm with her own ideas of pride in being black and to instill in him a sense of hard work. But he was attracted to the seamier side of Roxbury, Massachusetts, where they lived. Rather than enrolling at school in Roxbury, he started working as a shoe shiner. At seventeen, he lied that he was twenty-one and got a job as a railroad porter. His railroad travels enabled him to see Harlem, a black neighborhood in Manhattan, New York, for the first time; after he was fired from that job, he settled in Harlem.

In Harlem, Malcolm found it easier to say he was from Detroit than to try to explain where Lansing, Michigan, was. He soon acquired the nickname "Detroit Red" because of his red hair and reddish-brown complexion. He fell in with small-time hustlers and gamblers, got into trouble with both the police and the gamblers, and fled for his life back to Boston.

In Boston, Malcolm and some friends formed a burglary ring. For a while they were successful, but eventually they were caught. In February 1946, Malcolm was convicted of burglary and sentenced to ten years in prison. He was not yet twenty-one.

In prison, Malcolm was in such despair that he

didn't care about anything. He was so unruly that he spent most of his time in solitary confinement. He cursed everyone and everything, including God and religion. His unruliness and hostility earned him the nickname "Satan."

Then, after he had been in prison for two years, he received a letter from his brother Philbert. In it, Philbert told him that he had discovered the true religion of the black man, the Nation of Islam. Malcolm wrote a nasty letter back to Philbert. Then he received a letter from his brother Reginald. He was astonished to learn that all his brothers and sisters who were living in Detroit had become Muslims, followers of the Honorable Elijah Muhammad.

Although he was skeptical of any kind of religion, Malcolm was impressed by Philbert when he visited him in prison and by the letters he received from his other Muslim brothers and sisters. In spite of himself he wanted to believe in something, and the teachings of Elijah Muhammad attracted him.

One day, Malcolm sat down to compose a letter to Elijah Muhammad and was embarrassed about his lack of education—he had not gone past the eighth grade. In order to express himself better, he obtained a dictionary; in order to improve his handwriting, he started copying the words in the dictionary. Malcolm copied the entire dictionary! Now that he could understand the words in books, he began to read. He tried to find proof of Elijah Muhammad's teachings about the great history of the black man on earth, and in so doing he discovered the history of his own people.

No longer was Malcolm unruly and hate-filled. He

was too intent on learning, and on praying. He was released from prison for good behavior and immediately went to Detroit, where he moved in with his brother Wilfred and family. He learned how to apply the teachings of Elijah Muhammad to everyday life and attended Temple No. 1. He soon had the opportunity to meet Elijah Muhammad himself, who bestowed upon him the surname X to replace the "slave name" Little.

Malcolm X confided to Elijah Muhammad that he was troubled by the empty seats at temple services and asked for the opportunity to try to recruit new members. Given the go-ahead, he devoted himself to bringing the word to whoever would listen to him. He was so successful that membership in Temple No. 1 grew markedly; in 1953 Elijah Muhammad appointed him assistant minister of Temple No. 1.

But soon Elijah Muhammad announced that he had bigger plans for Malcolm X. As his emissary, Malcolm X was to travel to other cities, recruit new members to the Nation, and set up new temples. Within a few months, Malcolm X had established Muslim temples in both Boston and Philadelphia.

Malcolm served for a short time as minister of Temple No. 11 in Boston. During that time, he helped recruit Louis Eugene Walcott to the Nation of Islam.

6
Louis Farrakhan Joins the Nation of Islam

Although membership in the Boston Nation of Islam Temple No. 11 was probably only about 1,000, the Muslims were a presence in the city's black sections. The men stood proud and erect in their suits, starched shirts, and bow ties; the women in their long dresses and head scarves also showed pride and dignity. And their leader, the fiery Malcolm X, was on a mission to spread the word of Allah as conveyed by His messenger, Elijah Muhammad. He saw in Louis Eugene Walcott a talented young man who had the potential to be a leader. For his part, Louis Eugene Walcott saw in Malcolm X not only a strong black leader but a father figure.

And then he met Elijah Muhammad. He traveled to Chicago to attend a Savior's Day meeting, had an audience with Muhammad, and found the father he had lost at such a young age. He resolved immediately to devote his life to this great man. That meant giving up his music, for Elijah Muhammad said he would have to choose between music and Islam. He did so. It would be twenty years before he picked up a musical instrument again.

With Elijah Muhammad in Chicago, Malcolm X

took on the role of mentor to Louis Walcott, whom Elijah Muhammad renamed Louis X on his conversion. Soon, Louis X had adopted some of Malcolm X's mannerisms, such as the older man's habit, while concentrating, of holding his head in his left hand, thumb beneath his chin and index finger against his temple. He also imitated Malcolm's preaching style. For his part, Malcolm X was very proud to play the role of big brother to Louis X and made special efforts to help the younger man and his family. According to Benjamin Karim, a trusted assistant to Malcolm X, Malcolm "put shoes on his [Farrakhan's] feet when he first went to Boston, and food in his mouth."[1] In actuality, they never worked together for any extended period of time in the same temple, for in March 1954 Elijah Muhammad sent Malcolm X on to Philadelphia to start yet another temple. It took Malcolm X only three months to establish Temple No. 12 in Philadelphia, and the following month, Elijah Muhammad named him Minister of Temple No. 7 in New York City. But Malcolm X continued to guest-teach every week at Temple No. 11 in Boston, and the two remained in close contact.

In some ways, the two men were similar; in other ways, very different. Both were good-looking, light-complected, and bespectacled. Malcolm X was the taller of the two. Both were highly articulate, and both believed fervently in the teachings of Elijah Muhammad. Except for the important fact that both had lost their fathers at an early age—Malcolm X at six, Louis X at three—their backgrounds could not have been more different. Malcolm X had only an eighth-grade formal education; he'd been a small-time criminal and had spent time in jail. Louis Walcott had three years of college, had never been in trouble with the law, had a wife and family, and was earning a good living as a performer. And yet both had suffered the cruel realities of being black in America, of having the deck stacked against them at every turn. And both had responded to the message of black pride and black nationalism that was at the core of the teachings of the Nation of Islam.

Louis Walcott was part of a new type of African-American male that was being attracted to the Nation of Islam. Whereas most of the earlier members had been impoverished and ill-educated, and a substantial number had been former criminals, the incredible changes in their lives that membership in the Nation had wrought had not been lost on their more fortunate brothers and sisters. The black writer Stanley Crouch recalled in an article in the *Village Voice* in October 1985, "Suddenly here were all these clean-cut, well-dressed young men and women—men mostly. You recognized them from the neighborhood. They had been pests or vandals, thieves or gangsters. Now they were back from jail or prison and their hair was cut close, their skin was smooth, they no longer cursed blue streaks, and the intensity in their eyes remade their faces. They were 'in the Nation' and that meant that new men were in front of you, men who greeted each other in Arabic, who were aloof, confident, and intent on living differently than they had."[2]

Even middle-class black people were impressed, and more and more of them also sought out the Nation for that special pride that seemed to hang like an aura around its members.

Whereas Malcolm X joined the Nation as an individual, Louis X joined as a family man, and with his family. His wife shed the name Betsy Ross, with its echoes of the American flag, and her former Roman Catholic beliefs, and was given the name Khadijah X. His children also took Muslim names. For Louis X's wife and female children, Nation membership meant especially great sacrifices in some ways, for the Nation was very male-dominated. Elijah Muhammad preached submission of women to their husbands, although they were to be treated with respect. They were not to work outside the home, but instead to concentrate on making the home a place of rest and peace for their husbands and children. Single women were of course welcome in the Nation, but while they were expected to work as teachers at the various Universities of Islam and in the restaurants, stores, and other businesses the Nation started, they could never hope to become officials in the movement.

Malcolm X was a more charismatic speaker than Louis X, but he was older and more mature. Louis X had his own talents to contribute to the movement. He wrote and recorded a song, "A White Man's Heaven Is a Black Man's Hell," which soon became a favorite Nation of Islam anthem. And he also wrote two plays containing the message of the Nation, which were performed at mosques across the country, usually on the same bill.

In *The Trial*, a white man guarded by two black policemen faces an all-black jury as a black prosecutor delivers the charges:

"I charge the white man with being the greatest liar on earth! I charge the white man with being the greatest

**Malcolm X, shown here addressing a Nation of Islam conven-
tion in Chicago, was a charismatic speaker with a zealous
commitment to Elijah Muhammad and the Nation of Islam.
He built the membership of the Nation of Islam dramatically
and made it a national movement, attracting young men like
Louis Eugene Walcott along the way.** (AP/Wide World Photos)

drunkard on earth. . . . I charge the white man with
being the greatest gambler on earth. I charge the white
man, ladies and gentlemen of the jury, with being the
greatest peace-breaker on earth. I charge the white man
with being the greatest adulterer on earth. I charge the
white man with being the greatest robber on earth. I
charge the white man with being the greatest deceiver

on earth. I charge the white man with being the greatest trouble-maker on earth. So, therefore, ladies and gentlemen of the jury, I ask you, bring back a verdict of guilty as charged."[3]

The jury finds the defendant guilty as charged, the sentence is pronounced—"Death"—and the frightened defendant is dragged away, loudly protesting his innocence and listing all he had "done for the Nigra people."

In the second play, *Orgena* ("a Negro," spelled backward), black Americans are satirized as dope addicts, alcoholics, and flashily dressed businessmen and educators. The message is that this is what the white man has made of them. Near the end of the play, the Muslim faith and the teachings of Elijah Muhammad restore these "lost" people to the original dignity and intelligence they once had in their great civilization.

Louis X was clearly a rising star in the Nation of Islam. His first important position was as leader of the Fruit of Islam unit attached to Temple No. 11 in Boston. By this time, the Fruit of Islam no longer carried guns. Elijah Muhammad was much less militant and political than W. D. Fard had been. He did not believe in courting trouble, and having a group of armed men patrolling the black neighborhoods was to invite interference and downright hostility from mostly white police forces. As it turned out, the Fruit of Islam, dressed in suits and bow ties, with looks on their faces that dared anyone to start trouble, were able to keep the peace by their very presence.

Next, on the recommendation of Malcolm X, Louis X was appointed an assistant minister of Temple No. 11. Elijah Muhammad agreed that the young Bostonian was another natural leader who would help spread the message of the Nation of Islam.

Little information is available about the career of Louis X at Temple No. 7. But as a devout and committed follower of Elijah Muhammad, his story and that of the Nation as a whole were intertwined with that of Malcolm X, the man who almost single-handedly put the Nation of Islam on the map.

7
The Nation Takes Notice of the Nation

When Malcolm X arrived in New York City in June 1954, Temple No. 7 was a little storefront, and the entire Nation of Islam membership in the largest city in the country would not have filled one bus. Malcolm X recalled in his autobiography, "Even among our own black people in the Harlem ghetto, you could have said 'Muslim' to a thousand, and maybe only one would not have asked you, 'What's that?' "[1] Malcolm X was appalled. Here was a city with over a million black people in its five boroughs. The potential for the Nation of Islam was unlimited.

Malcolm X found the worldly-wise and weary residents of Harlem difficult to approach. In the early months, he was continually frustrated. But he kept on. His single-mindedness about advancing the cause of the Nation was disturbed during this period when he fell in love with Sister Betty X, born Betty Sanders, who joined Temple No. 7 in 1956. A nurse, she taught Muslim Girls Training classes one night a week after her normal work at a local hospital. She and Malcolm X were married in January 1958, and in the next six years would have four daughters.

Betty X understood and shared her husband's sense of mission for the Nation; she did not mind all the traveling he had to do, even though it meant he had rare moments to spend with the family. He was determined to make inroads into Harlem's black population. He targeted the Christian church congregations by holding temple services at 2 P.M. on Sundays, so churchgoers could attend after their regular services. In his sermons, he preached against the white man's religion that promised black people heaven in the hereafter while the white man enjoyed heaven on earth. He visited prisons. He made speeches on street corners. Gradually, membership grew, and Temple No. 7 was able to open a restaurant, through which Malcolm X knew he could attract more members. But the real turning point came when New York Muslims showed their support of one of their number who was the victim of police brutality.

The incident occurred not long after Malcolm X and Betty X were married. One night on a Harlem street corner, two white policemen broke up a scuffle between two black men and ordered passersby to move on. When the passersby did not run away as the police expected, the police attacked them with their nightsticks. One of the victims happened to be Brother Johnson Hinton of Temple No. 7. His scalp was split open, and he was loaded into a police car and taken to the local police precinct house.

Hinton's companion, also a member of Temple No. 7, immediately called the restaurant to report what had happened, and within half an hour fifty members of Temple No. 7's Fruit of Islam, led by Malcolm X, had taken up positions in closed-rank fashion in front of the precinct house. The police tried to deny that Hinton was there, but Malcolm X demanded to see for himself what condition the man was in. Allowed in to see Hinton, Malcolm X insisted that Hinton be hospitalized, and the police summoned an ambulance. When the ambulance departed for Harlem Hospital, fifteen blocks away, Malcolm X and the Fruit of Islam followed on foot. The crowd that had gathered outside the police precinct house fell in behind them, and as the parade made its way along Lenox Avenue, others joined in. Reaching Harlem Hospital, the Fruit of Islam formed ranks as before. The rest of the crowd milled about, muttering angrily and threateningly about police brutality. When a police official told Malcolm X to "get those people out of here," Malcolm X informed him that his people were peaceful and disciplined and that the other people were not his problem.

Only after receiving the assurance of doctors at the hospital that Brother Hinton was getting the best care did Malcolm X give the order for the Fruit of Islam to disperse. The unruly crowd left also. The Nation of Islam later helped Hinton win a brutality suit against the New York City police; but the immediate effects of the show of force were more important to Malcolm X. The story of how the Muslims had stood up to the police made headlines in the weekly *Amsterdam News,* and between those who had actually witnessed the event and those who read about it, the word about the Muslims finally got out in Harlem. Offered a weekly column in the *Amsterdam News,* Malcolm X eagerly accepted. His column was then taken over by Elijah Muhammad himself, and Malcolm X began to write one for the *Her-*

ald Dispatch in Los Angeles, where he was engaged in establishing a new Muslim temple. Malcolm X also founded a Nation of Islam newspaper, *Muhammad Speaks.*

From Harlem, word about the Muslims spread quickly to the rest of the city. It was not long before Mike Wallace, then a young television news reporter who had a program called "Newsbeat" on local television station WNTA, became interested in the Nation. With Louis Lomax, a black veteran news reporter, as chief researcher, Wallace undertook an investigation of the Nation of Islam. The program aired on July 10, 1959, and included footage taken at mosques and Muslim-owned-and-operated restaurants in New York, Chicago, and Washington, D.C., as well as clips of a performance of Minister Louis X's *The Trial* before an audience of 2,000 black people at Boston's John Hancock Hall. The program also presented excerpts from Elijah Muhammad's speeches and those of other ministers, including Malcolm X, and an interview with Malcolm X that Louis Lomax conducted after flying to Chicago to secure Elijah Muhammad's consent.

The program was called "The Hate That Hate Produced," a title suggesting that white hatred of blacks had produced black hatred in response. But its emphasis was on the anti-white teachings of the Nation of Islam. Malcolm X complained later that every phrase he had uttered in his interview had been edited to produce the greatest shock value. Whether or not the program presented a balanced picture of the Muslims, it sent shock waves through New York, whose white newspaper editors and columnists sounded the alarm about this group of black segregationists and black supremacists. From there, the national newsmagazines carried the story to the rest of the country; soon, the Nation of Islam was nationwide news.

It was quite a different story about African-Americans than those that people around the country had been reading in the last few years. By 1959, five years after the landmark U.S. Supreme Court ruling in *Brown v. Board of Education*, the direct-action civil rights movement had riveted the attention of the nation and begun the career of the man who would come to be regarded as the greatest civil rights leader in U.S. history, Dr. Martin Luther King, Jr. The direct-action civil rights movement of the 1950s had started when black people in Montgomery, Alabama, had boycotted the city's buses after a woman named Rosa Parks had been arrested after refusing to give up her seat to a white man. The black bus riders of Montgomery had remained off the buses for more than a year as the case had proceeded from local to state to federal courts and then reached the highest court in the land, the U.S. Supreme Court. At last, in late 1956, the Court ruled segregation on public transportation unconstitutional.

Martin Luther King, Jr., had served as president of the Montgomery Improvement Association, which had kept the boycott going by encouraging the city's black population to stay off the buses, urging them to remain nonviolent and not react in kind to the violence being done to them by whites who wanted the boycott ended, and by raising money for vans to transport people to and from their jobs. Hoping to build on the victory in Montgomery, King had then joined with other black southern ministers to form the Southern Christian Leadership Conference (SCLC). Its first major action was to hold a Prayer Pilgrimage in Washington, D.C., to demand the right to vote for black people, who were usually prevented from voting in the South because of literacy tests, poll taxes, and other requirements aimed at denying them a political voice.

The repercussions from the television program "The Hate That Hate Produced" were still being felt across the nation in February 1960 when students from the black North Carolina Agricultural and Technical College in Greensboro staged a sit-in at a local Woolworth's lunch counter. They were soon joined by white students from other local colleges, and within weeks the student sit-in movement had spread like wildfire around the South. Martin Luther King, Jr., and the SCLC had helped the students form an organization of their own, the Student Nonviolent Coordinating Committee (SNCC, pronounced "Snick"), that would engage in direct-action civil rights tactics but follow the philosophy of nonviolence.

Soon, older civil rights organizations were considering waging their own direct-action campaigns— marches, sit-ins, boycotts, and the like. There was an overwhelming sense of mission to finally right the wrongs of slavery.

All these efforts were aimed at achieving integration, not separatism—at inspiring the majority white population to at last live up to the democratic principles on which the United States was founded. The more moderate black leaders felt constrained to disavow the Nation of Islam as representing only a tiny segment of

America's black population. This infuriated the Muslims.

As Minister of Temple No. 7 in New York, the media capital of the world, Malcolm X was the representative of the Nation of Islam to whom reporters turned most often for responses to what the rest of the country was saying. After discussing what he should say with Elijah Muhammad in Chicago, he responded with the fury he felt: "For the white man to ask the black man if he hates him is just like the rapist asking the *raped*, or the wolf asking the *sheep*, 'Do you hate me?' The white man is in no moral *position* to accuse anyone else of hate!"[2]

At a Muslim rally in New York City, Malcolm X belittled the integrationist goals of moderate black leaders and preached complete separation of black people from white America.
(AP/Wide World Photos)

In response to what the moderate black leaders were saying, he was equally scathing. He called them "black bodies with white heads" and charged that they were mere puppets for whites. He belittled their integrationist goals: "No *sane* black man really wants integration! No *sane* white man really wants integration! No sane black man really believes that the white man ever will give the black man anything more than token integration. No! The Honorable Elijah Muhammad teaches that for the black man in America the only solution is complete *separation* from the white man!"[3]

In 1961, two years after "The Hate That Hate Produced" aired on New York television, C. Eric Lincoln's book *The Black Muslims in America* was published. Lincoln, who in 1956 was teaching religion and philosophy at Clark College in Atlanta, Georgia, had been struck by a student's paper on the incompatibility of the Christian religion with the black man's aspirations for dignity and equality in America. On questioning the student, he learned that the young man had come under the influence of the local Muslim minister. Lincoln undertook a study of the Nation of Islam and produced the first book about the movement. The term "Black Muslims" was Lincoln's; Elijah Muhammad, Malcolm X, and other Muslim ministers took great pains to correct the impression that they called themselves Black Muslims: They were black *people*. They were properly called Muslims. But the name stuck.

The Black Muslims in America inspired another huge response from the public, and once again Malcolm X was thrown into the spotlight as the official spokesman of the Nation of Islam and its National Minister.

8
The End of Malcolm X

The Nation of Islam benefited from all the publicity generated by "The Hate That Hate Produced" and *The Black Muslims in America*. Taking advantage of the increased recognition, Elijah Muhammad appeared at a number of mass rallies in cities with Muslim temples; caravans of buses carried the Muslim faithful to the rallies. Thousands attended, and many more were unable to fit inside; huge speakers were set up outside the rallies so they could hear the speeches.

Malcolm X was always present; his role was to prime the crowd before he introduced the Honorable Elijah Muhammad. So were his brothers, Wilfred, minister of the temple in Detroit, and Philbert, minister of the temple in Lansing, Michigan, and Elijah Muhammad's son, Wallace Muhammad, minister of the Philadelphia Temple. By this time, there were also temples in Los Angeles; Atlantic City; Washington, D.C.; Camden, New Jersey; Richmond, Virginia; Hartford, Connecticut; and Buffalo, New York. Louis X was one of the youngest ministers, but he was not the only one who had grown up middle class. One minister was a former Christian cleric; another was a pathologist. They reflected the increasingly middle-class membership of the Nation of Islam.

The Nation still held a strong attraction for poorly educated prisoners, who were lured by its discipline and the hope it held out for turning one's life around. But the strong discipline emphasized by the Nation and its emphasis on a close family life also had appeal for law-abiding black people. So did its stress on black self-help, as reflected in the growing number of businesses started by Muslims in cities with active temples. Elijah Muhammad preached self-reliance and self-determination. He called for a separate black nation to be carved out of the United States and was engaged in buying up land in the Midwest with a view toward one day realizing that goal. His way was to turn the back of the Nation to the nation and go it alone, and this appealed to middle-class blacks who had had to be twice as good and work twice as hard as whites to achieve. Some of the Nation's official beliefs, such as the story of the evil scientist Yakub, were treated with private skepticism, but the idea that Christianity was a white man's religion that kept the black man down struck home to many. They were tired of trying to fit in; they believed integration would never work.

These conclusions were diametrically opposed to the hopes of the majority of African-Americans. Except in Atlanta, the South's largest city, the Nation of Islam had made few inroads in the South. Southern blacks, subjected to the cruelest forms of segregation, were also, as a group, the most strongly Christian. They believed that America could be better and that through the application of Christian principles and nonviolent protest tactics, they could overcome the hatred that festered in white souls. While the Nation of Islam was holding mass rallies in northern cities, Martin Luther King, Jr.'s, Southern Christian Leadership Conference, the Congress of Racial Equality, the Student Nonviolent Coordinating Committee, and the National Association for the Advancement of Colored People were conducting Freedom Rides to test laws against segregation on interstate bus travel, voter registration drives and marches for voting rights, and boycotts of businesses that discriminated against blacks.

A. Philip Randolph, founder of the Brotherhood of Sleeping Car Porters, the first African-American labor union, believed the time had come for a massive March on Washington for Jobs and Freedom. He managed to persuade the leaders of the major civil rights organizations to support the march, and brought in white labor and church leaders as well. Scheduled for August 28, 1963, the march was planned to be the largest peacetime demonstration in U.S. history.

The Nation of Islam would not be participating. Malcolm X voiced the Nation's belief that the major civil rights leaders were but "puppets" of the administration of President John F. Kennedy and that the march was really a pep rally in support of the president. Two days before the march, Malcolm X arrived in Washington, D.C., and announced that he would hold a press conference to explain his views on what he called the "Farce on Washington." The conference was to be held August 27, on the evening before the march.

Worried that if he denounced the march on the eve

On August 27, 1963, a quarter of a million people, young and old, black and white, converged peacefully in the nation's capital for the March on Washington for Jobs and Freedom, the largest peacetime demonstration in U.S. history up to that time. (AP/Wide World Photos)

of the event he might succeed in persuading some people to stay away, the civil rights leaders met with Malcolm X and asked him not to hold the planned press conference on August 27, arguing that he would be going against the entire black community if he did. Malcolm X agreed not to hold the press conference as originally planned. He did hold a press conference during the march, and did indeed denounce it. But because of the rescheduling, the conference did not affect participation in the march; nor was the conference well-attended, because most reporters were covering the march itself. The march was a huge success, attracting at least a quarter of a million people, black and white, and making a powerful statement to America and its elected representatives in the nation's capital. In less than two years, laws would be passed that would effectively end legal segregation in the United States.

Malcolm X had compromised his own position for the good of the black community. He had not been in the habit of doing so. But by 1963, he had come to recognize some deep divisions between his beliefs in what the Nation of Islam could become and what Elijah Muhammad wanted it to be.

In the view of Malcolm X, the Nation had the potential to use its numbers and influence to right the wrongs committed against blacks by white society. But that was contrary to Elijah Muhammad's strict policy of nonengagement. Malcolm had heard the Muslims criticized because they talked tough but never *did* anything, and part of him agreed with that sentiment. Muslims were not to vote or engage in any types of political activity or civil rights demonstrations. In Boston, Minister Louis X

severely criticized a temple member just for joining a
community group that protested police brutality against
African-Americans.[1] In doing so, Louis X was toeing the
anti-engagement line established by Elijah Muhammad.
Malcolm X's sister, Ella, had left the Boston Muslim
temple in 1959, partly because its leaders refused to
participate in activities that she felt would benefit the
community.

Far more serious than this disagreement over tactics, however, were events that occurred in the early
1960s—events that shook Malcolm X's faith in himself,
in Elijah Muhammad, and in the Nation of Islam. Ever
since he had become a national figure, Malcolm X had
been aware of growing jealousy of him within the movement. Elijah Muhammad continued to support and encourage him to his face, but the younger man was aware
that privately Elijah Muhammad might be concerned
that he was becoming too popular. If Malcolm X's faith
in Elijah Muhammad had not been shaken at that time,
he might have been able to withstand the jealousy and
bad feeling. But Malcolm X was beginning to be convinced that rumors he had heard since as far back as
1955 might be true. It was whispered that Elijah Muhammad, in addition to fathering nine children by his
wife, had also fathered several children by various secretaries over the years. In July 1962, two of his former
secretaries filed paternity suits against him.

There was no stronger prohibition in the Nation of
Islam than that against adultery. It was difficult for
Malcolm X to believe that the man he had idolized all
these years could have committed such a sin. Even
when he learned for himself that the charges were true,

Malcolm X could not turn his back on his mentor. With the help of Wallace Muhammad, Elijah Muhammad's son, Malcolm reviewed the Qu'ran and the Bible to remind himself that other important figures in religious history, such as David and Lot, had committed similar sins. Malcolm X told himself, and began to teach at Temple No. 7, that a man's accomplishments outweighed his personal, human weaknesses.

But the rumors continued. They were especially rife in Chicago and Detroit, where the Nation of Islam began to lose members, and where some non-Muslim blacks were becoming adamantly anti-Muslim. Before the rumors reached the East Coast, Malcolm X decided he had better prepare some of the ministers there. He was in for a surprise. As he recalled in his autobiography, "I found then that some of them had already heard of it; one of them, Minister Louis X of Boston, as much as seven months before. They had been living with the dilemma themselves."[2]

Then, on November 22, 1963, President John F. Kennedy was felled by an assassin's bullet while riding in a motorcade in Dallas, Texas. The nation was in shock. Elijah Muhammad immediately sent out a directive that no Muslim minister was to make any comment whatsoever on the assassination. Malcolm X fully expected to obey that directive. But then Elijah Muhammad canceled a planned speech in New York City and asked Malcolm X to take his place. After the speech, a reporter asked him his opinion on the president's assassination, and without thinking, he responded that white people's hate had finally cut down the nation's president, that it was a case of "the chickens coming home to roost." The next day, that remark screamed from news headlines and news broadcasts. At his regularly scheduled monthly meeting with Elijah Muhammad that same day, Malcolm X learned that his remark would have an adverse effect on all Muslims and that he was to be silenced for the next ninety days. He was not to talk to the press, or teach at Temple No. 7. Louis X was named National Minister in his place.

Malcolm X soon understood that he would never regain the support and trust of Elijah Muhammad. He learned that one of his own assistant ministers was saying he should be killed, and he knew that in the tightly disciplined world of the Nation, such talk could have been approved by only one man. After a trusted assistant told him of a plan to wire the ignition of his car with a bomb, Malcolm X knew his time in the Nation of Islam was over. He announced that he was leaving the Nation.

While his faith in Elijah Muhammad was shattered, Malcolm X continued to believe in many of the tenets of the Muslim faith he had learned. He still believed in Allah. He called a press conference in New York and announced that he was forming a new organization, called Muslim Mosque, Inc., with temporary headquarters at the Hotel Theresa in Harlem.

To understand what Allah meant for him to do, Malcolm X decided to make a pilgrimage to Mecca, an act that all true believers in the world Muslim faith are expected to undertake at least once in their lifetime. The pilgrimage was a revelation to him, for he found that there were many white Muslims who had no racism in their hearts. He concluded that what was wrong with

America was not white people themselves but the social and economic system in which they had been brought up. "America needs to understand Islam, because this is the one religion that erases from its society the race problem," he said.[3] He converted to the Sunni branch of the world Muslim faith and took a new Muslim name, El-Hajj Malik El-Shabazz. On returning to the United States, Malcolm X renamed his organization the Organization of Afro-American Unity and announced that it would work for human rights for African Americans through a program of militant black nationalism. Instead of nonviolence, the OAAU would stress active self-defense against white racists. While this policy was not in accordance with the beliefs of Dr. Martin Luther King, Jr., King and Malcolm X were now able to come to an understanding.

In July 1964, Malcolm X again traveled abroad, staying away for eighteen weeks and spending much of that time in Africa. His meetings with various African leaders led him to conclude that the concept of black nationalism was too confining, for it left out, among others, Algerians who were fighting for their independence against the French.

Just before Malcolm X flew back to the United States from Africa, *Muhammad Speaks*, the newspaper he had founded, ran a series of scathing editorials against him. One of them, a five-page article, was written by Minister Louis X, once one of Malcolm's most loyal followers, whom Malcolm often called "little brother." He was Malcolm's enemy now. There were rumors that he had been bought off by Chicago with the offer of a new house in Boston. But Louis X proba-

Dr. Martin Luther King, Jr., and Malcolm X in March 1964. By that time, Malcolm X had broken with the Nation of Islam and could see ways in which he and the more moderate civil rights leader could work for common goals. (AP/Wide World Photos)

bly did not need to be bribed to take the side of Elijah Muhammad, who was an even stronger father figure to him than was Malcolm. In the December 4 issue of the newspaper, Louis X used a musical analogy to challenge his former mentor: "Is Malcolm bold enough to return and face the music—since he ordered the notes to be played—after bowing out and leaving the musician with untrained dancers?" The article compared Malcolm X with various hypocrites in Islamic history, charged him with using his "venomous poison to wash Messenger Muhammad with mud and filth," and called him "the great liar and scandalizer of his master."

Then came a stark and open call for the assassination of Malcolm X:

"Only those who wish to be led to hell, or to their doom, will follow Malcolm. The die is set, and Malcolm shall not escape, especially after such evil, foolish talk about his benefactor [Elijah Muhammad] in trying to rob him of the divine glory which Allah has bestowed upon him. Such a man as Malcolm is worthy of death and would have met with death if it had not been for Muhammad's confidence in Allah for victory over the enemies."[4]

Meanwhile, the Nation of Islam went to court to secure an order of eviction against Malcolm X and his family, whose home in the New York City borough of Queens was owned by the Nation. A rash of death threats came to him by telephone, and at least three times he and his followers were confronted by armed Muslims. On February 13, 1965, his home was hit by gasoline bombs while he and his family slept; no one was injured.

Although Malcolm X was beginning to wonder if government forces, such as the FBI, might somehow be in on the plot, there was no question in his mind that Muslims were deeply involved in a conspiracy against him. At one point, he told reporters that he knew the names of five Muslims who had been assigned to kill him and that he would announce them at the next OAAU meeting.

On Sunday, February 21, 1965, as he spoke from the stage of the Audubon Ballroom in Harlem, Malcolm X was shot by two men. Three men, all members of the Nation of Islam, were later convicted of his assassination. A total of five men were directly involved in the plot, all of them from the Muslim mosque in Newark, New Jersey. Louis X was at the Newark mosque that day. He claimed he was on his regular rotation schedule of teaching and preaching as Elijah Muhammad's Na-

The body of Malcolm X was buried in a cemetery in West-chester, New York, as his widow, Betty Shabazz, looked on (at right). Assassinated by Black Muslims on the stage of the Audubon Ballroom in Harlem on February 21, 1965, Malcolm X died before he was able to put his new Organization of Afro-American Unity on a firm footing. (AP/Wide World Photos)

tional Minister. But in the minds of many, including Malcolm X's widow, Betty Shabazz, that was too great a coincidence. Everyone knew that Louis X had sided with Elijah Muhammad against Malcolm X; everyone had read, or heard about, Louis X's editorial in *Muhammad Speaks* calling for Malcolm X's assassination. Although Louis X was never arrested for alleged involvement in the plot to kill Malcolm X, many Muslims and others believed he shared responsibility for the murder.

In addition to his widow, Malcolm X left behind six daughters, two of whom, twins, had not yet been born. Two of the little girls, six-year-old Attallah and four-year-old Qubilah, on the stage with their father when he was gunned down, were old enough to have some terrified understanding of what had happened. It would mark their lives forever.

When Malcolm X was assassinated, the majority white press dismissed him as a militant who had little following. An editorial in the *New York Times* the day after his death described him as a twisted man who had turned "many true gifts to evil purpose," had a "ruthless and fanatical belief in violence," "did not seek to fit into society or into the life of his own people," and was killed by someone who came out of the "darkness that he spawned."[5]

But the attitude of the *Times* editors and of many others soon changed. Around the end of October 1965, *The Autobiography of Malcolm X* was published. Told to the writer Alex Haley, who later wrote the landmark book *Roots*, it was an honest look at Malcolm X's own life and development. Wrote Eliot Fremont-Smith in his review of the book in the *New York Times* on November 5, 1965, "As this extraordinary autobiography shows, the source of Malcolm X's power was not alone in his intelligence, energy, electric personality or ability to grow and change, remarkable as these were. Its source was that he understood, perhaps more profoundly than any other Negro leader, the full, shocking extent of America's psychological destruction of its Negroes (which he calls 'an almost automatic function of white society')." Fremont-Smith also noted in his review the increasingly prevalent opinion among civil rights advocates that with the death of Malcolm X blacks had lost "their most able, articulate and compelling spokesman."[6]

Malcolm X was an outspoken, charismatic black man who articulated the anger and hope of many black people. He died before he was able to formulate a strong new program, and the sense of what might have been has pervaded his memory ever since. What if he had lived? What kind of movement would he have been able to form? How might it have made the lives of African-Americans different? One of the greatest tragedies of his death was that the legacy he left was incomplete. One of the greatest triumphs of his life was that his memory continues to grow, his life to be celebrated— not just in the film *Malcolm X* by Spike Lee, or by the wearing of "X" rings and baseball caps and T-shirts, but by people who read his autobiography and yearn to have known him, or to have been alive during his lifetime, or to have heard what he had to say in the last year of his life.

Even Louis Farrakhan, whom some suspect of having been involved in the assassination, now says, "But today, looking back, Malcolm would be much more valuable to us alive."[7]

9
The Nation Torn Apart

The departure and subsequent assassination of
Malcolm X threw the Nation of Islam into chaos. Temple members left in droves. Elijah Muhammad's son,
Wallace, named after Wallace D. Fard and said to have
been the chosen one who had an aura around him as
the most strongly spiritual son, split with his father. He
returned to the fold, but would leave two more times
before his father's death in 1975.

In the meantime, there was trouble among Muslims
in Boston. In his years as Minister of Temple No. 11 in
Boston, Minister Louis X had established a reputation
for rigid adherence to Muslim doctrine and the rules of
discipline laid down by Elijah Muhammad. But the verbal attack on Aubrey Barnette over Barnette's joining a
community group protesting police violence against
blacks started a series of events that led to an embarrassing moment for the Nation of Islam.

Barnette was a graduate of Boston University with a
job at the post office, where he worked overtime to save
for his future. But he was expected to devote so much
time to the Nation of Islam that he was forced to stop
working overtime; in addition, contributions to the tem-

ple consumed twenty percent of his income. After being verbally chastised by Minister Louis X, he was even more unhappy in the Nation, and he wrote a letter to Temple No. 11 announcing his decision to leave the mosque, lest his unhappiness affect others.

Nine months later, in January 1965, Barnette happened to be at a Boston airport only fifteen minutes after Muslims had made an attempt on Malcolm X's life. The police, who were immediately called by Malcolm X's bodyguards, rounded up anyone who "looked suspicious," and briefly detained Barnette for questioning. Shortly afterward Barnette was beaten, probably because the Muslims who saw him with the police assumed he was testifying against them. Barnette called the beating an act of revenge for his having left the Nation.

Far from frightening Barnette into keeping his mouth shut, the beating made him angry enough to go to the media with his story. In February 1965, the same month as the assassination of Malcolm X, *The Saturday Evening Post* contained an article written by Barnette with a reporter named Edward Linn titled "The Black Muslims Are a Fraud." In it, Barnette told of the outrageous demands for time and money placed on Muslims. He detailed how businessmen who became Muslims were forced to give up their businesses for lack of time. He exposed the quota system governing the sale of copies of *Muhammad Speaks*, explaining that mosque members were supposed to pay for the copies of the newspaper even if they did not sell them. According to Barnette, "When a brother fell too far behind, members of the terror squad [the Fruit of Islam] would pay him a night visit. If he still wouldn't—or couldn't—get up the money, they would invite him out for a ride, drive him to Franklin Park and work him over."[1] The use of such terror tactics had caused many Muslim business-men to leave the mosque in protest, according to Barnette.

Barnette detailed other incidents of terror by the Fruit of Islam, one involving relatives of the wife of Minister Louis X. According to him, Captain Clarence of the Fruit of Islam received information that the brother and brother-in-law of the minister's wife, both of whom were members of the Fruit of Islam, were tak-ing karate classes at a local YMCA (Young Men's Chris-tian Association), which was strictly out of bounds for Muslims. When questioned, the two men insisted that they had only been trying to find out whether karate was worth teaching to the rest of the Fruit of Islam. Captain Clarence did not believe them and ordered his lieuten-ants to beat them.

The publication of Barnette's article in a national magazine so close to the death of Malcolm X was highly embarrassing for the Nation of Islam, and especially for Louis X, in whose mosque the incidents Barnette re-ported had occurred. But no lasting damage was done to Minister Louis X. He had a relationship with Elijah Muhammad similar to that which Malcolm X had once enjoyed, and after the defection of Malcolm X he and Muhammad had grown even closer.

Elijah Muhammad named him Minister of Temple No. 7 in New York to replace Malcolm X; he also se-lected Louis as National Minister, a special position that Malcolm X had once occupied. As National Minister,

Louis X introduced Elijah Muhammad at the annual Savior's Day events, as Malcolm X had done. Also as National Minister, Louis X attended and addressed the pan-African Congress that was held in 1970.

Minister Louis X strictly toed the line laid down by Elijah Muhammad. He strove to avoid public controversy. He refused to give interviews. He concentrated on shoring up the membership of the Harlem mosque and reestablishing the discipline that had been lost in the upheaval after Malcolm X's departure.

Louis X also embraced the ambitious new goals that the Nation of Islam announced in the late 1960s and early 1970s, which set forth an economic program that would be a giant step from the small restaurants, bakeries, and clothing stores the Muslims had concentrated on earlier. The new plans were to buy up land and establish large farms in the South, a medical complex in Chicago, and a large fish-importing business. To finance these operations, there was talk of applying to the federal government for funds from minority economic development programs, such as the Office of Economic Opportunity and the Small Business Administration. As Elijah Muhammad's National Minister, and as a supporter of the new economic thrust, Louis X traveled widely to meet with local community-development programs, black banks, and black insurance companies.

It is believed that this ambitious economic program was spearheaded by Elijah Muhammad's son, Wallace Muhammad. Elijah Muhammad was in his seventies and feeble by this time. Traditionally, Elijah Muhammad had prohibited contact with the government. Whoever was behind it, the program proved to be unrealistic. The idea of seeking federal loans was soon dropped, for the traditionally secretive Nation was unwilling to open its books for the kind of rigorous outside inspection required of those who received federal money. The mostly poor and working-class membership of the Nation could not support such ambitious projects as a medical complex or a fish-importing business, no matter how large a percentage of their income they tithed or how many copies of *Muhammad Speaks* they sold. In 1972, the government of Libya came forward with a $3 million "loan" to the Nation, which caused great controversy, for Libya was considered a terrorist state. But the loan was only a stopgap measure for the Nation's economic plight.

The Nation of Islam experienced other problems in the early 1970s. There were tensions within the Nation as members realized their aging leader would eventually die and wondered who would succeed him. Discipline was not as tight, and in the early 1970s there were a series of violent incidents involving Muslims.

These were violent times in America. In the South, despite the passage of federal laws aimed at guaranteeing equal rights to blacks, racist whites resisted the changes in their lives. When the Student Nonviolent Coordinating Committee tried to register voters in rural Mississippi and Alabama, its workers and their local black associates were beaten and murdered. In April 1968, Dr. Martin Luther King, Jr., was assassinated in Memphis, Tennessee, where he had gone to assist striking black sanitation workers. The following June, Senator Robert F. Kennedy, brother of the late president, was assassinated in Los Angeles.

Blacks in northern urban ghettos, largely unaffected by the civil rights movement in the South, rioted in many cities in 1964 and 1965. There was a turning away from the philosophy of nonviolence by even some of its staunchest former proponents, among them leaders of the Student Nonviolent Coordinating Committee (SNCC). (AP/Wide World Photos)

This violence had already been evident in urban areas for years. Blacks in northern urban ghettos had been largely unaffected by the civil rights movement in the South. Many young blacks in those areas had never bought in to the idea of nonviolence, and they were angry over the continued lack of opportunity in education and jobs, over police brutality, over the fact that triumphs in the area of civil rights law had done nothing to improve their lives. Simmering tensions had erupted in several northern cities in the summer of 1964—including New York City; Rochester, New York; Jersey City, Paterson, and Elizabeth, New Jersey; and Philadelphia—causing death and injury to scores of people and millions of dollars in property damage. In 1965, an even worse riot occurred in Watts, a black section of Los Angeles. In the summer of 1966, Martin Luther King, Jr., and the Southern Christian Leadership Conference had tried to take their tactics of nonviolent protest to Chicago to improve conditions there, but they had been unable to inspire a significant following.

In 1966, the Student Nonviolent Coordinating Committee, brutalized in their attempt to register voters in the South, foreswore nonviolence, ejected its white membership, changed its name to the Student National Coordinating Committee, and announced a new "Black Power!" agenda. In California the same year, two young black men formed the Black Panther Party, which stressed militant self-defense along with a program of economic development. In several cities, confrontations occurred between former loyal followers of Malcolm X and Muslims who regarded him, and them, as traitors.

The increasing militancy among competing groups of blacks erupted in violence in several instances. In Philadelphia, Pennsylvania, in 1970 the Uhuru Kitabu bookstore, operated by former members of the Student Nonviolent Coordinating Committee, was firebombed after its operators refused to remove a Malcolm X poster from the store's window. In Atlanta in 1971, Muslims and Black Panthers fought over turf rights to sell their respective newspapers on a street corner.

The strife over Malcolm X erupted in New York's Temple No. 7 in 1972, when a shoot-out that began in the mosque spilled out into the streets. New York City police entered the mosque, an act that shocked the Muslim community, who regarded their temple as sacred.

By the early 1970s, world Islam had made greater inroads in the African-American community. The most famous convert was the basketball star Lew Alcindor, who joined the Hanafi Muslim sect and changed his name to Kareem Abdul-Jabbar.

By the early 1970s, Elijah Muhammad was old and frail. He spent most of his time in a house built for him by his followers in Arizona; the dry climate there was deemed better for his health. Louis X often visited him, knowing that the old man would soon die and desperately trying to continue the father-son relationship he had enjoyed for nearly twenty years.

At Elijah Muhammad's request, Louis X again took up music. Twenty years earlier, the leader had told his young convert that he would have to choose between music and Islam. But now he asked that Louis X play for him. Louis X bought a violin and began practicing long hours in the middle of the night when he was free of his ministerial duties, for the twenty-year layoff had made his playing skills rusty. But when Elijah Muhammad died, he put it aside again, not to take it up for nearly another twenty years.

The man Muslims called The Messenger died in early 1975, almost ten years after Malcolm X was assassinated. Leadership of the Nation of Islam, whose membership at the time was estimated at more than 50,000, passed to his son, Wallace, who changed his name to Warith. Although father and son had had their differences over the years, the elder man had concluded that Wallace was the best heir to his position of leadership. Muhammad had expelled Wallace from the Nation ten years earlier but had taken him back. For his part, Wallace had rejoined the Nation still convinced that many of its tenets and practices were wrong but determined to bring about change from the inside. Following Elijah Muhammad's death, the Muslim hierarchy chose Wallace to succeed his father.

Wallace, now Warith, Muhammad, had firsthand knowledge of world Islam and knew that the religion his father had propounded was far from true Islam. He wasted no time in putting an end to the false ideas of the divine nature of W. D. Fard and Elijah Muhammad, downgrading Fard from the status of Allah incarnate and his father from that of Messenger. Both, he taught, were ordinary human beings. He admitted the truth of his father's adultery and divided the inheritance left by his father among all the children, both legitimate and illegitimate. He disbanded the Fruit of Islam, hoping in that way to purge the Nation of its violent elements. He

On the death of Elijah Muhammad in 1975, his son, Wallace, who took the more Muslim-sounding name Warith, succeeded to leadership of the Nation of Islam and moved it toward orthodox Islam. (AP/Wide World Photos)

renamed the Nation of Islam the World Community of Islam and changed the name of *Muhammad Speaks* to *Bilalian News*, after a fourteenth-century Muslim. He sold off many of the Muslim restaurants, bakeries, clothing stores, and dry-cleaning establishments to pay off the Nation's debts and concentrated on the spiritual side of Islam rather than on economic self-determination. He took a proactive stand on political and community involvement, urged his followers to join community organizations, told them it was their responsibility to get involved in the political process, and even endorsed a presidential candidate, Jimmy Carter of Georgia, in the 1976 election. He put an end to the false ideas of racial separatism, the evil scientist Yakub, and the coming Armageddon that would set the darker world against the whites. He even announced that whites would be welcome at the Islamic mosques. A supporter of

Malcolm X, he renamed the Harlem mosque in Malcolm X's honor.

With every change, Warith Muhammad lost followers. Even those who had not believed in some of the more outrageous teachings missed the days when the Nation of Islam was nationalist, separatist, and feared by whites. Some disagreed with the deemphasis on economic power in favor of spiritual investigation. Members left the World Community, whose name was later changed to the American Muslim Mission, in droves.

Minister Louis X left, too. At first, he had supported the changes Warith Muhammad had instituted—at least publicly. Summoned to Chicago by Warith Muhammad, he had gone, fully prepared to help usher in the new era. But as membership declined and the financial power of the organization waned with the sale of so many of its businesses, he saw an opportunity to stake his own claim to leadership of the old-style Nation of Islam. After working with Warith Deen Muhammad for two years, he left the organization. He then spent almost a year without an organization of any kind, traveling in Africa, the Middle East, and Asia in what he called a period of spiritual "sleep." Then, in 1978, he resurfaced, having changed his name to Louis Abdul Farrakhan and prepared to reclaim the Nation of Islam.

He started a new newspaper, *The Final Call*, a name he had resurrected from early copies of a newspaper that Elijah Muhammad had put out in Chicago in 1934. The name refers to the call to black people to return to Allah as incarnated in Master Fard and his Messenger Elijah Muhammad. In it, Farrakhan wrote editorials exhorting Muslim "purists" to join him in rebuilding the original movement. He managed to raise the $3 million necessary to buy from Warith Muhammad's group the two most important buildings in the former Nation of Islam—Chicago Mosque No. 2 and Elijah Muhammad's mansion in the Kenwood section of Chicago, near Hyde Park. The ornate mansion had been built by Elijah Muhammad in 1972 as his official residence and the Nation's headquarters, although by then Muhammad was spending most of his time in Arizona to protect his health. From this physical base, Farrakhan then reestablished the Nation of Islam under the old rules. He reaffirmed the divinity of Elijah Muhammad and all that the late Messenger had taught.

Former Nation of Islam members had a clear choice between the American Muslim Mission of Warith Muhammad and the new Nation of Islam under Louis Farrakhan. What follows is a comparison between the basic beliefs of the two, as set forth by the Institute of Islamic Information and Education in Chicago. The III&E refers to the belief system of the Nation of Islam as Farrakhanism.

Allah, in Islamic belief, never appeared in any physical form. In Farrakhanism, Allah appeared in the person of W. Fard Muhammad in July 1930, the long-awaited "Messiah" of the Christians and the "Mahdi" of the Muslims.

Muhammad, in Islamic belief, is the last prophet and the last messenger of Allah; no other prophet or messenger will come. In Farrakhanism, Elijah Muhammad was the "Messenger of Allah." It is not clear whether it is possible for other messengers to come.

In Islamic belief, the Qu'ran, or Koran, contains

laws revealed to the Prophet Muhammad and is the last revelation of Allah to mankind. The Bible is recognized as the laws revealed to prophets and messengers from Moses to Jesus, but corrupted over time. The authenticity of statements in the Bible are judged by the Qu'ran. According to Farrakhanism, "We, the original nation of the earth . . . are the writers of the Bible and Qu'ran. We make such history once every 25,000 years . . . it is done by twenty-four of our scientists."

Islam requires prayer five times a day. Farrakhanism does not require this daily prayer ritual, but Friday is a major day for temple attendance.

Islam requires fasting during the month of Ramadan, the ninth month of the Islamic calendar, which is based on the lunar calendar, Farrakhanism requires fasting during the month of December.

Islam requires that every true believer make the hajj, or pilgrimage to Mecca, once in a lifetime, provided that his or her finances, health, and safety of travel permit it. Farrakhanism does not require the hajj.[2]

There are other differences. In general, world Islam does not impose strict dress codes, although women are to dress modestly and cover their heads. Farrakhanism reflects the rigid dress codes laid down by Elijah Muhammad. Men must wear the hair on their head close-cropped, must be clean-shaven, and must always dress in suits and bow ties. Women must wear long dresses and cover their heads with scarves. They must not wear lipstick or other makeup or heels over 1.5 inches.

Louis Farrakhan revived, or perpetuated, the call for a separate black state for African-Americans. Elijah Muhammad had demanded this separate territory also.

Like Elijah Muhammad before him, Louis Farrakhan was never specific about which area of the United States he had in mind.

To spread his message, Louis Farrakhan traveled hundreds of thousands of miles around the country during the late 1970s and early 1980s, speaking to black audiences. One of the first things he did was to reinstate the Fruit of Islam, and in his speeches he would make a special show of pointing to the members of the Fruit of Islam who always accompanied him, emphasizing their erect posture, clean-cut look, suits, white shirts, and bow ties, and then say to the audience, "You have gone back to drinking alcohol, smoking reefers, eating pork, and boogie-ing," he charged. "All the progress we made has been lost. The brothers are back on the street shooting dope and dying. The sisters are on the street corners hookin' for the white man. . . . Black families are breaking up at an unprecedented rate and black women and children are left unprotected because there is no man around."[3]

Farrakhan also continued to criticize Malcolm X, whose memory remained strong in the black community. At a "Welcome Home Brother Farrakhan" rally in Harlem in May 1980, Farrakhan said, "Yes, I even stand on Malcolm X. If Malcolm had not made the turn that he did, I would not have a guide to keep me from making the same mistake. He was an example for me instead of me being an example for him. He knew one day that I would be the National Representative. Because he died I have a chance to live."[4]

Regarded as a usurper by many former Nation of Islam adherents, Farrakhan did not attract a membership anywhere near that of the American Muslim Mission. In 1984, his following was estimated at about 10,000, ten times less than that of Warith Muhammad. But Farrakhan was soon to attract a larger following and become a national figure for his outspoken indictment of white America, very much as Malcolm X had before him.

10
Farrakhan and Jackson

Like Elijah Muhammad and Warith Muhammad, Louis
Farrakhan was convinced that black economic self-
reliance was crucial. This conviction led him to establish
close ties with the Reverend Jesse Jackson, a Chicago-
based activist whose organization, Operation PUSH
(People United to Save Humanity), worked to induce
large corporations to enter into agreements to hire black
managers, contract with black vendors, deposit in black
banks, and recruit black franchises.

Jackson, an ordained Baptist minister, had been an
aide to Dr. Martin Luther King, Jr., and had been with
King when he was assassinated. Charismatic and convinced of the moral rightness of his crusade, which he
couched in Christian terms, he did not, on the surface,
have much in common with Louis Farrakhan. After all,
Operation PUSH had begun as a program of King's
SCLC, and when the Reverend Ralph David Aberna-
thy, a close associate of King's, had succeeded to the
leadership of the SCLC and announced he would pur-
sue King's dream, Farrakhan had publicly scoffed,
"Talking about dreaming someone else's dream! Don't

you know that when you're dreaming, you're *asleep! Wake up*, black man!"[1]

But both Farrakhan and Jackson saw black people as victims of the American political system. In fact, their relationship had begun back in 1972 when Jackson had called a press conference to protest the entry of police into the Muslim mosque in New York. Both saw the American racial struggle in economic terms, and while one prayed to the Muslim Allah and the other to the Christian God, both had a strong sense that they were morally right and specially chosen to lead their people out of misery.

When in November 1983 Jesse Jackson announced his candidacy for the 1984 presidential election, Louis Farrakhan made his first foray into politics and supported him. He even registered to vote. When Jackson first declared his candidacy, he was not considered a major contender and was not given Secret Service protection like the major candidates. Farrakhan offered to have the Fruit of Islam, which he'd reestablished, act as Jackson's bodyguards until Jackson was finally given Secret Service protection.

Farrakhan often accompanied Jackson on the campaign trail, warming up audiences before the candidate appeared. Jackson sometimes referred to Farrakhan as his "surrogate," by which he meant that he considered Farrakhan worthy of appearing in his place.

Jackson campaigned as a spokesman for the poor and downtrodden of all races. He had founded a political party called the Rainbow Coalition, and in his formal announcement of his candidacy in Washington, D.C., the day following President Reagan's signing into law

When the Reverend Jesse Jackson campaigned for the 1984 Democratic presidential nomination, Louis Farrakhan got involved in electoral politics, an activity in which Muslim participation had always been noticeably absent. On February 9, 1964, he and his wife, Khadijah, registered to vote for the first time in their lives. (AP/Wide World Photos)

Martin Luther King, Jr.,'s birthday as an official national holiday, he made it clear that his candidacy was not for blacks only: "I would like to use this candidacy to help build a new rainbow coalition of the rejected that will include whites, blacks, Hispanics, Indians, Native Americans, Asians, women, young people, poor people, old people, gay people, laborers, small farmers, small-business persons, peace activists and environmentalists. . . . Together, the old minorities constitute a new majority. Together we can build a new majority. . . ."[2]

Jackson's message was welcomed by many Americans, including some whites. But a substantial portion of the Jewish community in the United States was against him because of his support of the Palestine Liberation Organization. In 1979, Jackson had traveled to the Middle East to meet with PLO leaders, who represented the refugees who had been forced from their lands when the state of Israel was created in 1948. He had hoped to talk also with Israeli leaders to try to persuade them to support the PLO's mission to carve out a homeland for the refugees. He was rebuffed by the Israelis but welcomed by Yasir Arafat, leader of the PLO; and when the two embraced, the photograph went around the world. Most American Jews had no intention of supporting a man who embraced the leader of a group that had used terrorist tactics against Israel and its people.

Early in December 1983, during a raid on Syrian antiaircraft guns in Lebanon, an American plane was shot down and its pilot, Lieutenant Robert O. Goodman, an African-American, taken hostage. Syria's president, Hafez el-Assad, saw the opportunity to make an example of the pilot, and refused to release him. Jesse Jackson believed he could use the contacts he had made in the Middle East during his 1979 trip to secure Goodman's release. Louis Farrakhan also had contacts in the Middle East that he had made on his trips there. He assisted Jackson in making plans for the trip and accompanied him to Syria. The day following Jackson's meeting with Hafez el-Assad, the Syrian foreign minister announced that Goodman would be released.

Goodman and Jackson returned to the United States as heroes, one as a military hero, the other as a diplomatic hero. Jackson's success in dealing diplomatically

Jesse Jackson succeeded in gaining the release of Lieutenant Robert O. Goodman, the U.S. Navy pilot shot down over Lebanon in December 1983. Louis Farrakhan (not shown) traveled to Syria with Jackson to negotiate Goodman's release. (AP/Wide World Photos)

in the Middle East, that unpredictable area of the world where so many American officials had failed, made him a viable political candidate.

Lieutenant Goodman just happened to be from New Hampshire, the state where the first presidential primary election is traditionally held. Jesse Jackson's success in obtaining Goodman's release helped him rise in the polls among the state's voters. But just eight days before the primary a story broke in the press that would have grave implications for Jackson's showing in New Hampshire.

Milton Coleman, an African-American reporter for the *Washington Post*, overheard and reported a remark Jackson had made in private conversation. Jackson had referred to Jews as "Hymies" and to New York City as "Hymietown." Coleman's article caused a furor among Jews, who had been suspicious of Jackson and critical of his visit to Syria and his embrace of PLO leader Yasir Arafat. Around the same time, a Jackson campaign office in Garden Grove, California, was firebombed. Although Garden Grove police found no evidence that the act had been committed by Jewish militants, many, including Louis Farrakhan, believed that it had. At a Jackson campaign rally on February 25, Farrakhan said, "Sit down, Jewish leaders, and talk with us. We are ready to sit down and talk like intelligent people who have a future at stake. . . . But if you harm this brother, I warn you in the name of Allah, this will be the last one you harm."[3]

Although Jackson apologized for his "Hymietown" remarks, it seemed impossible for him to quiet the furor. Louis Farrakhan just made Jackson's problem worse.

Farrakhan broadcast a weekly, syndicated radio sermon from the Final Call Temple in Chicago. On March 11, 1984, he delivered a rambling, angry message in which he attacked Jackson's Jewish critics and warned anyone who wished him harm: "I say to the Jewish people, who may not like our brother, it is not Jesse Jackson that you're attacking. When you attack him, you attack the millions who are lining up with him. . . . If you harm this brother, I warn you in the name of Allah, that will be the last one you *do* harm."

Many blacks regarded Milton Coleman as a traitor because he had reported Jackson's remark. As quoted in the *Chicago Tribune*, Farrakhan said, "What do you intend to do to Mr. Coleman? At this point, no physical harm. . . . But for now I'm going to try to get every church in Washington, D.C., to put him out. Put him out. Wherever he hits the door, tell him he's not wanted. If he brings his wife with him, tell his wife she can come in if she leaves him. But if she won't leave him, then you go to hell with your husband. That he's a traitor and [if] you choose to sleep in the bed with a traitor of your people, then the same punishment that's due that no good filthy traitor, you get it yourself as his wife. One day soon we will punish you with death. You say when is that? In sufficient time."

He then went on to say, "[T]he Jews don't like Farrakhan, so they call me Hitler. Well, that's a good name. Hitler was a very great man. He rose Germany up from the ashes. . . . Now, I'm not proud of Hitler's evils against Jewish people. But that's a matter of record. He rose Germany up from nothing. Well, in a sense you could say there's a similarity in that we're rising our people up from nothing. But don't compare me with your wicked killers."[4]

These press reports caused a furor, especially among Jews. Jesse Jackson was in the uncomfortable position of claiming as a supporter a man who seemed to be doing his best to alienate a large segment of the American people.

Jackson knew quite well that no matter how much he tried to reach out to Jews and other Americans of European heritage, his most solid support was among black people. They liked the "give 'em hell" attitude of Louis Farrakhan, although they might not count themselves among his followers. Jackson realized that he risked alienating those people if he repudiated Far-rakhan.

At first, Jackson tried to distance himself from Far-rakhan, arguing that those who disagreed with Farrak-han's views should talk to Farrakhan himself. But he began referring to the Nation of Islam minister as a sup-porter, rather than a surrogate.

Farrakhan himself realized that he had damaged Jackson's position as a moral force. He said much later that he was also concerned about the public fight against Milton Coleman. On a "Donahue" show in 1990, he related that just after the Coleman incident, he had called the reporter and requested a meeting, but that Coleman's bosses at the *Washington Post* would not allow it.

On April 11, 1984, Louis Farrakhan went to Wash-ington, D.C., for a rare press conference. At the confer-ence, arranged by the *Washington Post*, he insisted that the press had distorted his words and quoted him out of context. "I want the world to know that the lives of Mil-ton Coleman, his wife and his family are sacred to me . . . ," he answered when asked about the reported threats he had made.

On Adolf Hitler: "He was indeed a great man, but also wicked—wickedly great." On what had been per-ceived as a threat against Jackson's life by Jewish mili-tants: "We don't carry any weapons, and we certainly cannot threaten the Jewish community. You are well armed to take care of any little cheap threat. I don't threaten you with us. I threaten you in the name of Allah. It is He who has decided that He will fight our battles, and it is He and the force and power of nature that will be brought to bear if anything happens to this brother."⁵

But Farrakhan's explanations did nothing to soften the words quoted from his sermon on March 11, and in some cases he only exacerbated the problem.

Although Jesse Jackson had the most to lose by refusing to sever his ties with Louis Farrakhan, he was not alone among African-American leaders in not wishing to alienate other blacks by repudiating the Muslim leader. Farrakhan was the keynote speaker at a prayer breakfast at a National Conference of Black Mayors held in St. Louis later that spring. In his speech, he warned against efforts by white Democrats to "lock Reverend Jackson out" of the Democratic presidential convention. Many in his audience responded with repeated shouts of "Amen."

The "Hymietown" remark, and the controversy that resulted, tarnished Jackson's campaign and he would not be allowed to forget it. He won only one primary election, in Washington, D.C., and had few delegates representing him at the Democratic nominating convention that summer. He had, however, become a nationally known figure, and he was determined to keep himself in the national spotlight while he prepared for a second run for the presidency four years later.

Another result of Jackson's 1984 campaign for the presidency was that it propelled Louis Farrakhan into national prominence. Although Jackson severed ties with Farrakhan in the wake of growing protests—his name would not again be linked with that of the Nation of Islam leader for more than ten years—Louis Farrakhan intended to use and build on that national exposure.

11
POWER

Louis Farrakhan decided to capitalize on his new national prominence to further his and the Nation of Islam's goals for black economic power. After the death of Elijah Muhammad in 1975, many of the Nation of Islam's business concerns had failed. In 1981, casting about for ways to revitalize the economic vision of the Nation, Farrakhan welcomed an idea brought to him by Alphonzia Wellington, president of a market-research company in New Jersey. Wellington's idea was for the Nation to enter the personal health and beauty products business, which at that time was a $2.5 billion market in America. Farrakhan was excited by the idea of putting money back into the black community by providing jobs.

Wellington's idea was to eliminate the need for middlemen in the business by organizing a subscription service. Members would order a required dollar amount of the products, sell them for a profit, and pocket about forty percent of that profit. Farrakhan formed an organization called POWER (People Organized and Working for Economic Rebirth), and set about lining up five black manufacturers to supply goods ranging from detergent to mouthwash to makeup. These suppliers included Johnson Products of Chicago, an old, successful, and respected black business, as well as newer companies such as Worlds of Curls in California.

Farrakhan then undertook an ambitious, multicity promotional tour across the United States. His economic message was simple: "We all have to realize that this country isn't going to give us anything," he explained, adding, "We're just going to have to do it the old-fashioned way; we're going to have to earn it."[1]

But soon, controversy over Farrakhan's anti-Semitism overtook the tour. Partly, this was a result of lingering fear and resentment over his anti-Semitic statements during the 1984 Jackson presidential campaign. But partly, too, it was due to his introducing anti-Jewish statements into his pitch for black economic self-determination. In speeches to black audiences, he made a point of tying hatred of Jews into his calls for black economic self-determination by charging exploitation of the black community by Jewish merchants.

"The Jews came at the turn of the century . . . into the black community . . . and they became strong nursing from the breast of the black community, growing up to disrespect the very breast that had nursed them to strength. . . . They know someday they will be punished for the bad things they have done to blacks. . . . They didn't apologize for putting my brothers and sisters to live in homes or apartments and charging them the highest rents. [They] don't apologize for setting up liquor stores when [they] don't drink much [themselves], feeding my brothers and sisters alcohol. [They] don't

apologize for sucking the blood of our poor people that
[they] might live well."²

With those words Farrakhan was striking a sore
point in the black community, for in the history of the
United States there were many years when most of the
businesses in black communities were owned by Jews.
Jews from Europe came to the United States without
a tradition of land ownership, owing to discrimination
against them in the lands of their birth. They had made
their living as peddlers and tailors and storekeepers. In
the United States, they did the same, and because of
discrimination by non-Jewish whites, were often barred
from communities. So they started their businesses in
black communities. In some cases, the neighborhoods
were immigrant Jewish. But these communities
changed over time: Jewish immigrants moved away, and
blacks and Latinos moved in, becoming a new clientele
for the Jewish businesses.

In the 1960s, in many black areas most of the apartment buildings were owned by Jews, as were most of
the stores. This caused resentment on the part of the
black residents. In some cases, Jewish landlords did exploit the black residents of their buildings, and Jewish
shopkeepers charged high prices. On the other hand,
Jews were probably quicker than most to protest discrimination and legal segregation against blacks because
of their own historical experience as outcasts. Jews contributed a great deal of money to civil rights organizations and made up a substantial proportion of the white
northern college students who took part in the direct-
action civil rights movement of the 1960s. Jewish students were a strong presence in SNCC, and one of the

most infamous incidents of the civil rights era was the murder of two Jewish students, Michael Schwerner and Andrew Goodman, and a black student, James Chaney, which was committed by southern white racists. The relationship between the two groups has always been complicated; Louis Farrakhan's statements opened up some old wounds.

A few commentators pointed out that they were, indeed, old wounds. By the 1980s, merchants in black neighborhoods were more likely to be newer immigrants. Farrakhan himself admitted to Barbara Walters in a "20/20" interview in 1994 that it was in the 1960s that many Jews were the merchants and landlords in the black community: "Today, it's the Arabs and the Koreans and others. . . ." But the charges of Jewish exploitation of the ghettos retained their power to inflame.

The promotional tour began in Detroit, Michigan, in January 1985, and ended in New York City in October. Everywhere he went, Farrakhan drew huge crowds, mostly of African-Americans. On September 14, he drew an audience of 15,000 to the Forum in Los Angeles. A small delegation of whites attended that rally. It was led by Thomas Metzger of San Diego, former head of the Ku Klux Klan in California, who had formed a new organization called White Aryan Resistance. The ten-member delegation was there as guests of the Nation of Islam and contributed $100 to support the Nation's cause. Questioned by reporters, Metzger stated that talks between his group and the Nation had been going on for about a year.

According to Metzger, there had been two or three occasions on which his group had supplied information to the Farrakhan people on the movement of Jewish terrorist groups, whom Farrakhan believed were intent on destroying Jesse Jackson's campaign for the presidential nomination. Those who knew history were struck again by parallels with Marcus Garvey's UNIA movement earlier in the century. Garvey, too, had met with a racist white group, the Ku Klux Klan, and discussed shared philosophies and goals.

In every city he visited, Farrakhan's appearance was

During his national tour in 1985, Farrakhan's visits sparked protests over his anti-Semitic statements. At Wesleyan University, some 600 students and faculty held a rally and vigil outside the university hockey rink, where Farrakhan spoke to about 350 people amidst heavy security in April. (AP/Wide World Photos)

preceded by renewed controversy over his anti-Semitic remarks in the tour and during the Jackson campaign of the previous year. Local Jewish leaders called on local black leaders to repudiate Farrakhan and what he stood for. Some black leaders did speak out against him, but others refused to do so, angered at having their agenda set for them and resistant to the notion that their attitude toward Louis Farrakhan had become a sort of litmus test for support from the white community. Still others eventually repudiated him, resulting in the charge that they had waffled.

In Los Angeles, Mayor Tom Bradley's refusal to repudiate Farrakhan's statement outright cost him valuable white, and especially Jewish, support in his campaign for governor against George Deukmejian. In Washington, D.C., Mayor Marion Barry waited months before finally criticizing Farrakhan.

By the time Farrakhan reached New York City, the last stop on his tour, controversy was raging. Commented Governor Mario Cuomo, "There is no question that the language Farrakhan uses, the ideas he espouses, ideas of hate and divisiveness and polarization, are precisely the things that could tear this country apart." He added that Farrakhan's aim was "to set people against people" in hopes that "we can destroy ourselves."[3]

City Clerk David Dinkins, who would later be elected New York City's first black mayor, stated flatly, "I find his blatantly anti-Semitic remarks offensive, and I condemn them." Democratic Congressman Charles Rangel voiced the opinion of many black leaders when he protested that blacks were expected to condemn fel-

low blacks, while whites were not called upon to react
to controversial statements by white leaders. "I would
not, if someone said Jesus Christ was a phony, go
around asking Jews to sign a statement to condemn
him," Rangel said on one occasion; and on another,
"There is a lot of concern among a lot of blacks that
they don't want to be told what to do, notwithstanding
the fact that they probably would have done it anyway."

The Reverend Calvin O. Butts, pastor of Abyssinian
Baptist Church in Harlem, would not denounce Farrakhan. Referring to Israel's refusal to impose economic
sanctions against South Africa to protest its policies of
racial separation, Butts asked, "If I jumped up and said
all Jewish leaders in the United States should denounce
Israel, how many Jewish people would join me in that?
I don't think many."[4]

Wilbert Tatum, editor of the New York *Amsterdam
News*, editorialized, "In many ways, black leadership is
being placed between a rock and a hard place in terms
of their response to Farrakhan and his cleverly devised
messages. On the one hand, he preaches love of blacks
for themselves, self-help, economic independence and
survival of our communities. Interspersed with this
message of survival there is also a message of hate—
hatred toward Jews."[5]

A spokesman for the Black-Jewish Coalition, organized the previous year, read a statement that said, "We
must recognize that while Minister Farrakhan speaks of
hope, economic empowerment and black self-help, his
message loses some credibility because of the anti-
Semitic remarks that he may make or has made in the
past. The Black-Jewish Coalition urges all New Yorkers

Farrakhan delivered a fiery speech before 20,000 people at New York's Madison Square Garden on October 7, 1985. Although on such occasions he always urged his audiences to join the Nation of Islam, membership in the Nation remained comparatively small. (AP/Wide World Photos)

to move beyond the attempt to polarize our communities and intensify our efforts to improve the economic and social conditions, including education, housing, justice and employment, for all New Yorkers, blacks and Jews alike."[6]

Few black leaders attended the rally on October 7, which filled the huge Madison Square Garden in New York City beyond capacity. Thousands of ordinary blacks did. Some were inspired by Farrakhan's economic message; others attended because they wanted to show support of Farrakhan against attacks by Jewish and some black leaders and by media commentators. Still others went because they wished to reapply to their own job situations what he said. But thousands did not attend, because they believed his fiery rhetoric only worsened relations between blacks and whites, or because they considered him to be all talk and no action. What was his program? What had the Nation of Islam really done for the black community?

The rally at Madison Square Garden, attended by an overflow crowd of more than 25,000 people, was far less about economics and black self-help than it was about Jews. Several speakers warmed up the audience before Louis Farrakhan appeared. Russell Means of the American Indian Movement struck the tone with "Never have you seen a movie or a play denigrating the Jewish people." When Louis Farrakhan finally did appear, he spent the first hour attacking Jews who had attacked him. Only occasionally did he relate his remarks about Jews to economics, as in, "There are black manufacturers in this country who are willing to make these products [detergents and soaps for black consumers], but did you know the Jews . . . are pressuring those black manufacturers not to make them?"[7]

Farrakhan delivered to his audience the message that the death and destruction prophesied by Elijah Muhammad would soon happen in America. He left his audience emotionally spent, but with few tools with which to help themselves economically.

Farrakhan had also managed to lose his five POWER suppliers, all of whom had pulled out by the end of his tour. They could not afford being tied to Farrakhan's anti-Semitism. Farrakhan refused to be cowed. "Mr. Johnson did us a favor," he said, referring to George Johnson, CEO of Johnson Products, who had cancelled his deal, "because when he wouldn't do it [produce POWER products] for us, we had to do it for ourselves."[8] Earlier in the year, Farrakhan had met with and secured from Libyan leader Colonel Muammar el-Qaddafi a $5 million, interest-free loan to be used as seed money for the new enterprise. Believing that there were more possibilities abroad, Farrakhan left New York City for Jamaica to begin another promotional tour, this time in the Caribbean, Africa, and the Far East.

In Jamaica, the birthplace and final resting place of Marcus Garvey, Farrakhan placed a wreath on Garvey's grave. Garvey, the father of the black self-reliance movement, had also started a host of businesses. But his enterprises had collapsed.

So, too, did POWER. After the initial five business suppliers had pulled out, forcing Farrakhan and his advisers to rethink the enterprise, they had decided that the name POWER was not appropriate for a corporate title. So a holding company was registered with the State of Illinois: Nationway Ventures International, Ltd. The decision was also made to go after a broader market, which is one reason why the name POWER was dropped, for it was deemed too closely associated with African-Americans. Farrakhan even predicted that eventually nonblack members of the sales force would outnumber blacks.

Instead of a subscription plan, the idea now was to sell products door-to-door, with representatives buying goods from Nationway and then selling them and pocketing the profits. By the summer of 1987, Farrakhan said that 1,500 people had signed on, thirty percent of the 5,000 he hoped to attract. But the enterprise failed. One reason was that it was urban-based, and door-to-door sales are generally not successful in cities, where people sometimes fear going into unfamiliar neighborhoods and where residents are unlikely to open their doors to strangers. Even established door-to-door sales enterprises were seeing a drop in profits. Louis Farrakhan's dream of self-sufficiency would, at least for the time being, have to remain a dream.

12
The Two Sides of the Nation of Islam

In 1991, a doctor told Louis Farrakhan that he had prostate cancer. He determined to overcome the condition and went to a mountaintop retreat in Mexico to fast and exercise and pray. Some time later, Mexican doctors declared him free of cancer. "They don't know if I ever had it," he told a reporter in 1993, "but if I did have it, I don't now."[1] Whether or not he ever had the ailment, Louis Farrakhan had faced his own mortality, and a subtle change seemed to come over him.

He picked up the violin again, and he hired a music teacher to coach him three hours a day. As in his youth, he turned to the music of composer Felix Mendelssohn, whom he was surprised to learn had been born a Jew, although he and his family had later converted to Christianity. As Farrakhan's sixtieth birthday, May 17, 1993, approached, he decided to mark it by giving a violin concert. Surprisingly, he planned to give the concert in a Christian church, and to invite a Jewish cantor to take part in the service. He also took to making surprise appearances at classical music competitions in Chicago and elsewhere.

Louis Farrakhan explained that he would "try to do

After a doctor told him he had prostate cancer, Louis Farrakhan seemed to soften a bit. He resumed playing the violin, and in May 1993, in celebration of his sixtieth birthday, gave a benefit concert as an effort at reconciliation between the Jewish and black communities. (AP/Wide World Photos)

with music what cannot be done with words and try to undo with music what words have done."[2] It was his way of making overtures of peace to the mainstream community, and more particularly to the Jewish community. "I am not this ugly fellow you would like to make people think I am," he told a reporter for *Newsweek* in 1993. "It's necessary for the garbage to be cleared away so that a new and better relationship can be structured between blacks and Jews."[3] Outside observers wondered if Louis Farrakhan was mellowing. The threat to his health, his own aging, and the sheer weight of all those years of stridency and hateful words may have combined to persuade him that hate didn't work. Some compared this seeming change in Louis Farrakhan to that which had come over Malcolm X at a younger age.

But most observers were skeptical that a real change had taken place in Louis Farrakhan, and certain that no matter how many sweet notes he played on the violin, they would never erase the damage done by his words—especially in a time of renewed strife between blacks and Jews.

The simmering resentments between the two ethnic groups erupted again in the early 1990s. In July 1991, at the Empire State Black Arts and Cultural Festival in Albany, New York, Professor Leonard Jeffries, chairman of the African American Studies Department of the City University of New York, charged that rich Jews had helped finance the slave trade. He also claimed that a conspiracy had been planned and programmed out of Hollywood in which Russian Jews, aided by Mafia money, had put together a system for the destruction of black people. In the ensuing uproar, Jeffries was removed from his chairmanship at the City University of New York. Although he was reinstated and awarded damages after a jury found that he had exercised constitutionally protected free speech, Jeffries eventually stepped down from his position voluntarily. But he had set off a new round of hostility between blacks and Jews.

Coincidentally, the following month the Crown Heights section of Brooklyn, New York, erupted in three days of anti-Jewish rioting after a Hasidic motorist accidentally killed a black child. More than eighty Jews were injured, and a rabbinical student, Yankel Rosenbaum, was stabbed to death. His accused killer, Lemrick Nelson, was later acquitted of the murder.

Two months after that, in October, the Historical Research Department of the Nation of Islam published a book titled *The Secret Relationship Between Blacks and Jews*, which purported to prove that Jews were guilty of "monumental culpability" for the evils of slavery and the slave trade. The same month, Khalid Abdul Muhammad was named National Spokesman for the Nation of Islam. Born Harold Moore Vann, Khalid Muhammad had been a member of the Nation of Islam for some fifteen years and had served as its minister of defense and as regional minister for the West Coast. Most recently, he had served as minister of New York's Mosque No. 7. He and other leaders in the Nation at once began to tout the book in speeches and in interviews in *The Final Call*, the Nation's newspaper.

The book was issued as a defense of Louis Farrakhan's anti-Semitic speeches and writings. In fact, the May 4, 1992, edition of *The Final Call* featured a photograph of Farrakhan holding up a copy of the book beneath the headline "I Have Been Vindicated." The book was based on reputable sources, but critics charged that it grossly misrepresented and misquoted them. In June 1992, the Simon Weisenthal Center issued Dr. Harold Brackman's refutation of *The Secret Relationship* under the title *Farrakhan's Reign of Historical Error*. In it, he stated that he could compile a book of quotations from the writings and speeches of Louis Farrakhan that would "prove" that Farrakhan was one of the chief anti-black racists of the twentieth century, citing Farrakhan's statements that young black men who did not join the

Nation were "savages," that blacks who disagreed with his philosophy were "handkerchief-headed Negroes," that blacks were guilty of expecting handouts from whites, and similar statements.[4]

Henry Louis Gates, Jr., chairman of Harvard University's Afro-American Studies Department, wrote a full-page opinion piece in the *New York Times* in July 1992 in which he called *The Secret Relationship* "one of the most sophisticated instances of hate literature yet compiled" and charged that "the book massively misrepresents the historical record, largely through a process of cunning selective quotation of often reputable sources."[5]

Louis Farrakhan defended the book in fiery tones when he spoke to black audiences. His tone was quite different when he was questioned by Barbara Walters on a "20/20" program that was aired on April 22, 1994: "[T]here are many Jews who do not know the role that some Jews played in the slave trade, and it was a prominent role. But whether it was marginal or prominent, the fact of the matter is Jews have succeeded in the world [and] blacks are at the bottom of the socioeconomic ladder."[6]

The controversy resulted in brisk sales of the book in black communities, and increased opportunities for Nation of Islam spokesmen to speak about the book.

In November 1993, Khalid Muhammad was invited to lecture on *The Secret Relationship* at Kean College in New Jersey. To the assembled group of black and white faculty and students, he called Jews "the bloodsuckers of the black nation and the black community." "The Jews like money," he continued, "and they have always been after money. They want nothing else but money. . . . It was the Jews, brothers and sisters, the so-called Jews, not only who crucified Jesus in a kangaroo court, but it was the Jewish prosecutor Maddox who prosecuted the Honorable Marcus Mosiah Garvey in a kangaroo court. Jews in the judicial system that worked against Mr. Garvey, and ultimately worked toward Mr. Garvey being deported from America. The so-called Jews. The hook-nosed, bagel-eatin', lox-eatin' impostor, perpetratin' a fraud, Johnny-come-lately, just crawled out of the caves and heels of Europe, wannabe Jew, not the true Jew. For you [blacks] are the true Jew. You are the true Hebrew. You are the true ones who are in line with Bible prophecy and scripture, so teaches the most

Named National Spokesman of the Nation of Islam, Khalid Abdul Muhammad took over the role of fiery hate speaker and made headlines with his anti-Semitic speeches. So incendiary were his remarks that for a time in 1994 he was relieved of his duties with the Nation of Islam. (AP/Wide World Photos)

Honorable Elijah Muhammad and the Honorable Minister Louis Farrakhan. You are the people of the Bible that fulfilled the Bible prophecies."[7]

This speech at a small New Jersey college by a relatively unknown official in the Nation of Islam went largely unnoticed at first. But the Anti-Defamation League noticed, and the following January, on the occasion of the celebration of Dr. Martin Luther King, Jr.'s birthday, the League ran a full-page ad in the *New York Times* giving the contents of the speech. It caused a furor. The Reverend Jesse Jackson denounced it as "racist, anti-Semitic, divisive, untrue, and chilling," and he called for Farrakhan to repudiate his National Spokesman. But Farrakhan refused. In a speech in Harlem, he charged, "They're trying to use my brother Khalid's words against me to divide this house. . . . They don't want Farrakhan to do what he's doing. They're plotting as we speak."[8]

By early February, however, as the controversy continued to grow, Farrakhan had changed his mind. At a news conference in Washington, D.C., on February 3, he announced that he was demoting Khalid Muhammad. "While I stand by the truths he spoke," said Farrakhan, "I must condemn in the strongest terms the manner in which he spoke them."[9] Nevertheless, at a Nation of Islam Savior's Day event at the University of Illinois in Chicago later that month, Khalid Muhammad was in the front row when Farrakhan said, "I had to rebuke him because I want him to be the great statesman he was born to be." And referring to Muhammad's remark that Jews were bloodsuckers, he said, "I didn't say it, Khalid did. Did he lie?" The audience roared back, "No!"[10]

But to Barbara Walters on the "20/20" program

aired in April, Farrakhan said, "It is not proper, in my judgment, to mock physical characteristics, cultural habits of another people."[11]

Muhammad still wasn't silenced, although the Nation of Islam has procedures for doing so. He continued to lecture in the same vein he had at Kean College until, in May 1994, after giving a speech at the University of California, Riverside, he was shot by a disgruntled former minister of the Nation of Islam, who also wounded four of his Fruit of Islam bodyguards. A crowd immediately set upon the assailant, James Edward Bess, and beat him, yelling "He works for the Jews," before the police were able to wrest him away. An investigation into Bess's background revealed that he had been expelled from the Nation's Seattle branch three years earlier for not living up to the group's strict standards of behavior. Because at that time Khalid Muhammad had been regional minister for the West Coast, speculation was that Bess had held a personal resentment of Muhammad.

Few who knew the inner workings of the Nation of Islam suggested that the attack on Khalid Muhammad reflected growing tensions within the Nation of Islam. They firmly believed that James Edward Bess had acted alone. But Louis Farrakhan's demotion of Khalid Muhammad in February had worsened a growing factionalism between radical and more moderate elements in the Nation.

Following his recovery, Khalid Muhammad remained loyal to Louis Farrakhan, but he continued to give hate-filled speeches, believing that the Nation of Islam was the only place for disaffected blacks. His following appeared to be the rougher, more violent element in the Nation of Islam. Louis Farrakhan made no further moves to publicly criticize him. In fact, Farrakhan may have decided that the presence of Khalid Muhammad was to his benefit, for in a good-cop/bad-cop scenario, he, Louis Farrakhan, came out as the good cop.

By contrast, Conrad Muhammad, who assumed the position as minister of New York's Mosque No. 7 after Khalid Muhammad was named National Spokesman, was seen as more moderate, appealing to the middle class. Born Conrad Tillard in St. Louis, he had spent most of his childhood in a black neighborhood in Washington, D.C. He lost contact with his biological father

Conrad Muhammad, shown here at right, listening to minister Don Muhammad of Boston at a press conference in New York in January 1994, was elevated to the position of minister of New York's Mosque No. 7 after Khalid Muhammad was named National Spokesman. Conrad Muhammad represented the more moderate side of the Nation of Islam and was more appealing to the black middle class. (AP/Wide World Photos)

after his parents were divorced, and did not become close with his stepfather after his mother remarried. He was converted to the Nation of Islam after he joined the Jesse Jackson presidential campaign in 1984 and heard Louis Farrakhan speak at a rally in Washington, D.C. For Conrad Tillard, it was like finding his father at last. In fact, he often used the word *father* when speaking of Farrakhan. He changed his name to Conrad Muhammad, and began to speak and move like the leader. Conrad Muhammad rose quickly in the ranks of the Nation, inspiring jealousy in some fellow Nation members. The primary criticism against him was that he was too soft.

On January 9, after a robbery was reported at the Harlem mosque, eight New York City police officers were injured in a brawl with a crowd of worshipers. Muhammad did not take what was considered to be a sufficiently hard line against the police force of the new administration of Mayor Rudolph Giuliani, and he was briefly suspended by the Nation. Not long afterward, however, Louis Farrakhan paid a visit to the Harlem mosque to support his young follower.

Louis Farrakhan does not encourage or condone infighting. He would rather keep strong, charismatic figures like Khalid Muhammad and Conrad Muhammad in the fold. He understands that infighting weakens an organization. But awareness of these frictions within the Nation of Islam has caused observers to wonder just who will succeed Louis Farrakhan when he steps down, or if something should happen to him. Those questions were asked repeatedly in the fall of 1994 after it was charged that Malcolm X's daughter, Qubilah, had plotted to assassinate Louis Farrakhan.

13

The Assassination Controversy and an Assassination Plot

In November 1992 *Malcolm X*, a film biography by the black filmmaker Spike Lee, was released. Several years in the making, the film helped inspire a renaissance in interest in Malcolm X. African-Americans by the thousands began to sport "X" jackets, hats, T-shirts, and rings. Spike Lee, the film's highly successful director, had inserted references to Malcolm X in several of his earlier films, including his most successful to that time, *Do the Right Thing;* but he was not the only African-American artist to do so.

More obvious were the lyrics of such rap and hip-hop artists as Chuck D., with Public Enemy, and K.R.S.-One, with Boogie Down Productions. Beginning around 1990, when the twenty-fifth anniversary of Malcolm X's assassination caused many blacks to begin reassessing his importance, they had started using Malcolm X's words in their songs, exposing a whole new generation to the slain leader's beliefs. Spike Lee gave these rap and hip-hop artists full credit for beginning the revitalization of Malcolm X. He claimed he simply started to build on what was already happening.

Lee believed that the real message of Malcolm X's

Filmmaker Spike Lee on opening day of his film *Malcolm X*, November 18, 1992. Lee's film biography helped to revitalize the image of Malcolm X. (AP/Wide World Photos)

life was personal growth. He had been an illiterate criminal, and he had educated himself while in prison. He had been a militant black nationalist, and he had learned that in the larger world the issue of racism was not as simple as he had formerly believed. Lee wanted to show this growth through film, and in so doing he wanted to send young blacks the message, as Malcolm X had tried to do, that education and personal growth were the real point of the life of Malcolm X. He visited Malcolm X's widow, Betty Shabazz, who agreed to act as a consultant on the film. She was concerned about the picture Lee would paint of the Nation of Islam. She did not like Louis Farrakhan, and believed his faction of the Nation had been responsible for her late husband's death.

Lee also visited Farrakhan, whose Fruit of Islam had provided security on the Brooklyn set of *Do the Right Thing.* Initially, Lee did not ask Farrakhan for this kind of protection, but he did want Farrakhan's assurance that his faction of the Nation would not try to disrupt or interfere with his film. Farrakhan gave the blessings of the Nation to the project. His major concern was how Lee would portray Elijah Muhammad.

Other black groups were not so supportive. Amiri Baraka, the poet and playwright who had been born LeRoi Jones and taken a Muslim name after converting to Islam, believed that Lee would downplay Malcolm X's radicalism and adulterate the message of Elijah Muhammad. When shooting for the film began in the streets of Harlem, Lee anticipated demonstrations against the project by Baraka's group or others, and he decided to hire the Fruit of Islam as a security force on the shoot. The Fruit of Islam managed to keep the local citizenry at bay, but an incident occurred that no one had anticipated and no one could stop. One day a driverless car crashed into the shoot, doing minor damage. It was scary for Spike and his crew to inspect the car later and discover that a brick had been lashed to the accelerator pedal. They never found out who had rigged the car.

Spike Lee also paid members of the Nation as consultants to give the actor Denzel Washington, whom Lee had chosen to play Malcolm X, a two-week training course in the principles and practices of the Nation. When it finally opened in November 1992, the controversial film proved to be a tour de force for Denzel Washington, but at three hours long it did not enjoy the box office success Lee had hoped for. Those who saw it learned a great deal about Malcolm X and the Nation of Islam, however, and learned, too, of the suspected involvement of Louis Farrakhan in the assassination. The film suggested that Malcolm X's assassination had been a conspiracy between the Nation of Islam and the FBI.

The controversy over Malcolm X's assassination was renewed. In an open letter to Farrakhan written by five African-American ministers of different denominations and published in Boston, the ministers asked Farrakhan: "Given that five members of the Newark mosque were identified as Malcolm X's killers by one of the assassins and that you were reportedly at the Newark mosque the day of the assassination, what responsibility do you bear for Malcolm X's death?"[1]

Louis Farrakhan moved quickly to answer such charges. He insisted in a speech in March 1994 that he had had nothing to do with Malcolm X's death. He did admit, however, that he was among those who "created an atmosphere that allowed Malcolm to be assassinated."[2] This controversy was the primary reason Farrakhan consented to be interviewed on "20/20," a sure sign that he felt he needed to defend himself in a large public forum. To Barbara Walters of "20/20," he stated, "I was in Newark at that time, the time of the assassination. It was my turn to be rotated into Newark to handle the preaching or teaching that day, and that is my reason for being in Newark."[3] He went on to say that Betty Shabazz had never claimed he was a plotter in the death of Malcolm X. But a few days after that interview was taped, and well before it was broadcast, Betty Shabazz did say that. In a rare television appearance on WNBC's "News Forum," a local news show in New York, Betty Shabazz was asked if she thought Louis Farrakhan had had anything to do with the death of her husband. "Yes," she replied without hesitation. "Nobody kept it a secret. It was a badge of honor. Everybody talked about it."[4] Her mother's words sent shivers down the spine of thirty-four-year-old Qubilah Shabazz. She was frightened that Farrakhan or his people might harm her mother if she kept saying such things in public.

Qubilah Shabazz, then four years old, had been sitting on the stage of the Audubon Ballroom that Sunday afternoon in February 1965 when a man in the front row had stood up and emptied both barrels of a sawed-off shotgun into her father's chest. With her three sisters, she had been pushed under a chair by her mother, who had then thrown herself upon the girls to protect them as two other men in the audience had opened fire. But she had seen it all, and she would never forget the terror and the tragedy. Although she was the second-oldest daughter (Attallah was six), she was the only one, according to her godfather, photographer Gordon Parks, who seemed to understand that her father would not come back. She pleaded with her mother not to leave her.

Afterward, Betty Shabazz had tried to make her daughters' lives as normal as possible. She had hidden her copies of *The Autobiography of Malcolm X*, which had been published after her husband's death, because the book included a picture of Malcolm X's bullet-ridden body; but the girls had found the books. She had raised them quietly in suburban Mount Vernon, New

York, in a house that friends and supporters had helped her buy. Betty Shabazz had gone back to school, earning a doctorate in education and getting a job at Medgar Evers College in Brooklyn. Qubilah attended a Lutheran grade school in Mount Vernon. When she was eight years old, she wrote the following lines about her father on an index card: "Malcolm X was a brave leader, he fought for rights for all black people. His black preachings were in everybody's heart. In 1964 he was at the autobaum [*sic*] preaching. And everyone was listening instead of falling asleep. Listening to his black word. Then for not long he was shot. He dyed, but his black beautiful soul is in every black person's heart."[5]

For high school, Qubilah enrolled at the United Nations International School in Manhattan, where she studied Arabic seriously and also became fluent in French. Other students knew that she and her older sister, Attallah, were daughters of Malcolm X, but there were many children of famous people at the school and she felt no pressure. On graduation, she was accepted at Princeton University, but she had a hard time there. Fellow students suggest that other black students at Princeton expected her to carry the mantle of her father. Qubilah Shabazz wanted to be left alone. In 1980 she moved to Paris, where she studied at the Sorbonne and worked as a journalist. A love affair with a man said to be African resulted in the birth of a son, whom she named Malcolm.

Soon after the birth of her child, she returned to the United States and lived in California, New York, and Philadelphia, before settling in New York. She held a series of jobs, including waitress, secretary, and telephone sales person, while dreaming of being a writer and a potter; but she was unable to root herself firmly, even in her new Quaker religion. She spent time in a mental hospital and succumbed on occasion to a drinking problem that had first surfaced in high school.

Her older sister, Attallah, an actress and theatrical producer, lectured often on her father, and her younger sister, Gamilah, was a rap singer who incorporated excerpts from Malcolm X's speeches into her lyrics. Malikah, one of the twins and an architect, spoke occasionally about her father's legacy. But Qubilah refused even to talk about her father.

The release of the Spike Lee film biography of her father must have reopened many old wounds. A United Nations International School alumni directory had been published earlier that year. Qubilah Shabazz looked up a former classmate named Michael Fitzpatrick. In high school, he had sported a Grim Reaper tattoo and talked incessantly about guns. His mother is Jewish, and while still in high school Fitzpatrick had been active in the Jewish Defense League and had been arrested in 1977 for the bombing of a Russian-language bookstore. He had not actually graduated from the United Nations International School, although his picture had been in the 1978 yearbook. Qubilah Shabazz had not seen nor talked to him since 1980. The alumni directory listed him as living in Minneapolis, Minnesota, but did not give a telephone number for him. Shortly before Memorial Day 1994, Shabazz called his mother, who passed the message on to her son.

Michael called Qubilah soon after. As the two talked about mutual high-school friends and Qubilah's troubles with her ten-year-old son, she confessed that she hated Louis Farrakhan and had dreamed for years of having him killed—even of participating in the act. She also expressed her fears for her mother's safety. Eventually Qubilah asked Fitzpatrick if he would kill Louis Farrakhan.

In 1978, an FBI agent whom Michael Fitzpatrick had met in connection with the Russian-bookstore bombing, had asked Fitzpatrick to infiltrate a Jewish Defense League splinter group called SOIL (Save Our Israeli Land), which was suspected of trying to disrupt the Camp David discussions between Israelis and Egyptians. Fitzpatrick had acted as an FBI informant against the group. He had then been enrolled in the federal witness-protection program. Later, he may have joined the Communist Workers Party and again served as an FBI informant. He became addicted to cocaine and entered a recovery program, moved to Minneapolis in 1985, and briefly took up with an anarchic group the following year. He later worked for several gold and rare-coin dealers and threatened to expose shady practices at one. He was arrested in late 1993 on charges of drug possession but managed to rebound again, joining Alcoholics Anonymous and finding new work as a gold and rare-coin dealer.

Within a day or so of Qubilah Shabazz's call, Fitzpatrick got in touch with his former FBI contact from the New York bombing case in 1978. By late July 1994, Michael Fitzpatrick had become an FBI informant against Qubilah Shabazz and was taping their telephone conversations. In the first taped conversation, on July 27, 1994, Qubilah Shabazz made clear that it was her fear for her mother's safety that motivated her to hatch the plot: "I do think that eventually he's going to in a very slick way have her killed. OK, so it's either him or my mother."[6] Michael Fitzpatrick said that he hated Farrakhan, too, adding that Farrakhan was "dangerous to my people."

In the course of forty calls, all of which were recorded, the two discussed the idea of killing Louis Farrakhan. Fitzpatrick asked for money for immediate expenses, but Shabazz did not send any. In early September, Shabazz moved to Minnesota, telling friends that she was going to marry Fitzpatrick. Fitzpatrick, driving an FBI car, picked up Shabazz and her son, Malcolm, and registered them at a local Holiday Inn. The room was equipped with a hidden video camera, and FBI agents were in the next room. After ten-year-old Malcolm was put to bed, Shabazz and Fitzpatrick had a forty-five-minute conversation about the assassination plot. Fitzpatrick said it would be easy and that it would be done in a month or so. Shabazz warned him that the longer he waited, the more she would have second thoughts. She gave him $250.

The following day, Shabazz and her son moved into housing arranged by a social services agency and then found an apartment south of downtown Minneapolis. She went on welfare and enrolled Malcolm in a Montessori school. She tried to reach Fitzpatrick, but was unsuccessful. He had moved from Minneapolis to St. Paul without telling her. He finally resumed contact with her in late October, and in early November told her that the assassination was all set up. But by this time, Shabazz was "afraid to have any involvement in it" and told him that until she'd had time to think, she was not giving Fitzpatrick "the go-ahead to do it."[7]

In late November, following a complaint that Malcolm might be neglected, the boy was removed from his mother, although he was subsequently returned and the complaint dropped as unfounded. On December 20, five days before her thirty-fourth birthday, Qubilah Shabazz was visited by FBI agents. At first she thought they wanted to talk to her about Malcolm. Then she learned that they wanted to talk to her about the assassination plot.

After a lengthy interview with FBI agents, Qubilah Shabazz signed a statement in which she admitted to plotting with Michael Fitzpatrick to kill Louis Farrakhan. On January 12, 1995, she was charged with nine counts of using the telephone and traveling interstate "in the course of hiring another person for murder."[8] Her trial was scheduled for May.

When the story broke in the media, it created a furor. Was it another case of "the chickens coming home to roost"? Louis Farrakhan did not denounce the daughter of his onetime enemy. In Chicago, he told cheering supporters that the "child I knew and held in my arms as a baby" had been used by government agents in a "diabolical scheme" to undermine him as "the voice of black America." For once, Betty Shabazz could find common ground with the man she had hated for thirty years. She told reporters that she was "appreciative and surprised by Minister Farrakhan, by his words, his patience, his generosity."[9]

Betty Shabazz came immediately to her daughter's defense. She took Malcolm to live with her and hired

Qubilah Shabazz leaves the Minneapolis Federal Building on Thursday, January 12, 1995, after making her initial court appearance. Shabazz was charged with trying to hire a hitman to kill Louis Farrakhan. (AP/Wide World Photo/Carolyn Stewart)

William Kunstler, a veteran defense attorney in radical causes. At the pretrial hearing on January 18, Qubilah Shabazz pleaded not guilty to the charges.

In the next three months, the public learned through media investigations the background of Michael Fitzpatrick and read portions of the transcripts of the telephone calls. It became clear that the defense would make a case that Shabazz had been "entrapped" by Fitzpatrick and the FBI and that the confession she signed on December 20 had been improperly taken without the presence of an attorney. Although federal prosecutors maintained that they had enough evidence to convict Shabazz, who faced ninety years in prison if found guilty, the fact that she did not have an attorney until after she had signed the confessions, coupled with the media hype and the old passions that the case had reawakened, caused the government to strike a deal with the defense.

On May 1, just days before her trial was to begin, Qubilah Shabazz appeared in federal court in Minneapolis and signed a statement that had been worked out between her attorneys and government prosecutors. In it, she agreed to accept responsibility for her involvement in the assassination plot, to spend three months in a psychiatric, drug, and alcohol treatment program, and to find a job. She would essentially be on two years' probation.

Outside the courtroom she told reporters that even this statement had been coerced, but that she had signed it because it was better than going to jail. She then asked to be allowed to return to her private life and to live it privately.

14
Farrakhan in the Fold

The assassination plot against him put Louis Farrakhan in the headlines again, and people wondered anew what made him tick, how he could be so reasonable on some occasions, so unreasonable on others. Louis Farrakhan as a personality and Louis Farrakhan as leader of the Nation of Islam were in some ways two separate people. As a power base, the Nation of Islam was not very effective. To be sure, Nation of Islam attempts to rid selected black neighborhoods of drugs and crime had been successful, and the appeal of the Nation to blacks behind bars continued to be significant. But the number of actual, practicing members of the Nation remained comparatively small.

For those Americans who were attracted by a faith that was less white than Christianity seemed to be, that stressed discipline and clean living, there was world Islam, which over the years had been making greater inroads into American society as the population of Islamic immigrants increased. The greater presence of Islam was evident in many cities. There were an estimated 1,500 mosques in the United States by the 1990s. Their membership comprised immigrants from Arab countries as well as from African countries where Islam is the main faith. It also included an estimated three million African-American Muslims. Unrest in the Middle East and terrorist acts by Muslim fundamentalists had created a backlash against Muslims. Mosques had been burned down and seriously vandalized after such incidents as the Oklahoma City bombing in April 1995, for which Arab terrorists were originally suspected, although the bombers turned out to be white supremacists. But as more and more practicing Muslims immigrated to the United States, world Islam became more of an ingredient in the American stew. In cities like New York, in a development that appeared strange at first, Muslims were settling in areas in which Orthodox Jews predominated. But the coexistence of these groups was not so odd when one realized how close the lifestyles of the two groups were—with their emphasis on family and community, daily religious rituals, and dietary restrictions.

With world Islam available as an alternative, it was unlikely that Louis Farrakhan's Nation of Islam would ever be a powerful force in American life. Even with its small membership, however, it gave Farrakhan himself an institutional base and justified his presence at meetings of leaders of other black organizations.

While there were those in both the black and white communities who said that Louis Farrakhan would have little influence if the media would just stop paying attention to him, others believed that he served a purpose that was as old as the history of African-Americans: He gave voice to the anger and pain of a disaffected people. There was little question that he was one of the most respected leaders among black youth, who yearned to have been alive when Malcolm X was standing up as a man to "the [white] Man." More and more, other black leaders invited him to take part in their meetings and conventions, even at the risk of alienating white supporters, because he did have a constituency that was not reflected in the small membership of the Nation of Islam.

In June 1994, Louis Farrakhan was invited into the moderate black leadership fold. The National Association for the Advancement of Colored People organized a National Black Leadership Summit, to be held in Baltimore, Maryland, that month, with a follow-up meeting scheduled for August. The Reverend Benjamin F. Chavis, who had been named executive director of the NAACP more than a year earlier, wanted the conference to bring together leaders who spoke for all segments of African America, and so he had called upon the heads of black service sororities, black businessmen, and black psychiatrists. Those invited included the Reverend Jesse Jackson; the Reverend Al Sharpton, a militant black spokesman from Brooklyn, New York; Representative Kweisi Mfume of Baltimore, head of the Congressional Black Caucus; Dr. Leonard Jeffries, the controversial City College Black Studies professor; Warith Deen Muhammad, son of the late Elijah Muhammad; as well as Louis Farrakhan.

Not everyone in the NAACP agreed with Chavis about inviting the more radical black leaders, like the Reverend Al Sharpton and Dr. Leonard Jeffries. The invitation to Louis Farrakhan spurred particular controversy. Benjamin Chavis insisted that all black leaders

Benjamin Chavis, then executive director of the National Association for the Advancement of Colored People (NAACP), at the microphones during a news conference at the end of the three-day meeting of African-American leaders in Baltimore in June 1994. He is flanked by Mrs. Rupert Richardson, far left, president of the NAACP; Benjamin Andrews, left, board vice-chairman; William Gibson, right, board chairman; and Louis Farrakhan. (AP/Wide World Photos)

should take part in the conference and that the NAACP would not be dictated to.

In the days before the conference, many commentators, black and white, wrote editorials criticizing Chavis for inviting Farrakhan. On the day of the conference, several Jewish groups demonstrated against his inclusion, and one placard carried by a protestor read "A Christian Against Hate." Farrakhan was angered by all the controversy. He considered himself a major black leader and a spokesman for a significant portion of the black community. He was accustomed to being vilified by whites, but the controversy among blacks had brought back memories of the furor that had erupted during the 1984 Jackson presidential campaign. During the conference's afternoon session he was soft-spoken, but when the assemblage moved to Bethel A.M.E. Church for the evening session, he spoke with fire in his voice. He called those whites who protested his presence meddlers in the affairs of the black family. "If I need to be brought into line or refined, who better to do it than my own family," he asked. "We don't get in your family business. You stay out of ours." Then, slashing the air with his hand, he warned that "there will be a war on any Negro leader who doesn't want to unite for the benefit of our people."[1]

The smaller discussion sessions during the three-day conference focused on particular issues of concern to the black community and were closed to the public. They did not, according to participants, produce any specific plan for improving the quality of life for African-Americans. But the Reverend Benjamin Chavis believed that the conference had been an important first step toward unity of purpose. And the Reverend Al Sharpton, considered a marginal black leader by many, who told reporters that the conference had produced more symbols than substance, added that the meeting could still prove to be a watershed for defining black leadership. "We got to know each other. That is very important, crucial. We clarified that we could work together on certain general points."[2]

If there was a loser as a result of the conference, it

was the Reverend Benjamin Chavis. Within months, he had been ousted as executive director of the NAACP. The primary reason was the revelation that he had used NAACP funds to pay off a woman staffer who had charged sexual harassment. But he did not enjoy the support of his board or that of most of the organization's members, and one reason may have been his departure from the traditional moderate stance of the organization in embracing Louis Farrakhan and other controversial personalities.

If there was a winner as a result of the conference, it was Louis Farrakhan. By inviting him, the NAACP in effect endorsed him. It increased his stature as a leader and made him appear more mainstream.

Then Farrakhan's sympathetic response to the plight of Malcolm X's child caused even Betty Shabazz to change her attitude toward him. This was an important development in Farrakhan's attempts to gain acceptance in the mainstream black community.

But the watershed event in the career of Louis Farrakhan as a national black leader came several months after that, with the largest gathering of black people in the capital of the nation, Washington, D.C.—the Million Man March.

15
The Million Man March

The idea of a massive show of unity by black men grew out of the National Black Leadership Summit in June 1994. It was Louis Farrakhan's idea, but Benjamin Chavis, Jesse Jackson, and others responded positively to it. Much of the discussion at the summit had been about the plight of the black family. Nation of Islam teachings held that the man was responsible for the family, and even those leaders who were less patriarchal in their attitudes could not deny that it was black men in America who were the most troubled group.

During the discussion sessions that followed the summit, Farrakhan and the other leaders who supported the idea of the march settled on the official purposes of the march, which were several. The chief aim was to reach out to African-American men, whom they considered the most "endangered species" in America. The average life expectancy of black men was nearly ten years less than that of white men. Black men were far more likely to die violently at an early age, were twice as likely to be unemployed as were white men, and had the highest crime rate of any group in the United States population. The Million Man March would be an expression of atonement in which black men would demonstrate their awareness that they were themselves responsible for much that afflicted their group. It would be an opportunity to apologize to black women and to God for not taking better care of their families. But the responsibility for atonement would not be solely on the shoulders of black men. The nation also had much to atone for in its treatment of them.

Another aim of the Million Man March was to assert the potential for black political strength. This assertion was especially important at the time. The United States seemed to be turning away from the sentiment that African-Americans and other poor people needed help. A new conservative philosophy was taking hold, one that was against affirmative action, welfare, Medicare, Medicaid, and other government programs that had traditionally provided a safety net for blacks and other poor people, including the elderly. Faced with huge budget deficits, even the Democratic president, Bill Clinton, wanted to cut back on social programs and to end "welfare as we know it." In the meantime, the Republican Party, which was in the majority in both houses of Congress, was asserting its political muscle. House Speaker Newt Gingrich outlined a program, which he called the Contract With America, that promised to cut taxes and reduce the deficit by eliminating or reducing many social programs. The Million Man March displayed the strength in numbers of black men—a strength with the potential of being marshaled in votes and political action against cutbacks in education, job-training programs, and other social welfare programs.

The title Million Man March meant just what it indicated: Women were not invited. In Farrakhan's view, and based on his adherence to the teachings of Elijah Muhammad, black men bore the chief responsibility for the black family, and thus for black life. Women's support was welcomed, but in behind-the-scenes roles, such as raising money to pay for buses to transport men to the capital.

The march was scheduled for Monday, October 16, 1995. One of the most crucial items on the organizational agenda was to publicize the march and its goals. To attract the target number of one million black men, they had to get the word out. The closing days of the trial of former pro football player O. J. Simpson, who was accused of the deaths of his ex-wife Nicole Brown Simpson and her friend Ronald Goldman, and the jury's verdict in the case, could not have come at a better time. First, Farrakhan reinserted his presence in the minds of the nation by offering his Fruit of Islam guards to protect Simpson's chief attorney, Johnnie L. Cochran, and members of Simpson's family during the days when attorneys for both the prosecution and defense made their closing arguments. And then the jury rendered its verdict.

Whichever way the verdict went, it would have been good for Louis Farrakhan and his Million Man March. Had Simpson been found guilty, the rage of many blacks would have spurred them to show their bitterness by joining a mass demonstration. But the not-guilty verdict was even better, for it was considered a triumph by many, a revenge against the racist white law-enforcement system. The Million Man March was the perfect vehicle to show solidarity by the population group that had suffered most severely at the hands of white police.

Within a week of the Simpson verdict, the mainstream media were concentrating on the Million Man March story, and Louis Farrakhan was everywhere on the television news programs. The more publicity the impending march received, the more national black leaders felt the need either to endorse or to criticize the march. Endorsing the march, in addition to Chavis and Farrakhan, were Washington, D.C., mayor Marion Barry and most of the members of the Congressional Black Caucus. Against the march was one member of the Congressional Black Caucus, Representative Gary Franks (Rep.) of Connecticut. General Colin L. Powell, another African-American much in the news at the time because of his recently published autobiography and wide speculation that he might consider running for the presidency, also distanced himself from it. Although he said he supported its goals, he declined to attend, citing the commitments of his book tour.

For all the talk of goals such as atonement and assertion of responsibility, the fact remained that the march had been Louis Farrakhan's idea and that he would be the keynote speaker at the event. In the minds of many, Louis Farrakhan remained a symbol of separatism, anti-white feeling, and particularly anti-Semitism. While the Reverend Benjamin F. Chavis, the national director of the march, insisted that "the message and the messenger have transcended all divisions in the black community,"[1] some of the major black leaders in the nation did not see it that way. The head of the 8.2-million member National Baptist Convention told his followers not to attend, as did Warith Deen Muhammad, still regarded as the leader of the largest group of black Muslims in the country. The National Urban League and the National Association for the Advancement of Colored People declined to participate.

Four days before the march, the Anti-Defamation League, an influential national Jewish organization, took out a large ad in the *New York Times* with the headline "What If a White Supremacist Called for a March on Washington?" The ad went on to say, "If this happened, no matter what the cause, no matter how legitimate the issue, no one could ignore the fact that a hatemonger was the driving force behind the march. The same is true of Minister Louis Farrakhan and the Million Man March. . . . Unfortunately, this March will be the largest event led by an anti-Semite in recent American history. And that cannot be ignored."[2]

Three days before the march, five well-known black women called a press conference in New York City to denounce it. They included Angela Y. Davis, philosophy professor at the University of California at Santa Cruz and a symbol of 1970s black radicalism; Marcia Gillespie, editor-in-chief of *Ms.* magazine; Paula Giddings, an author and historian; Jewell Jackson McCabe, founder of the Coalition of 100 Black Women; and Luke Harris, a professor at Vassar College who had recently organized African-American Agenda 2000, whose aim was to bring together men and women to combat racism, sexism, and homophobia. Among their criticisms was the march's virtual exclusion of women. "Justice cannot be served," Davis read from the group's prepared statement, "by countering a distorted racist view of black manhood with a narrowly sexist vision of men standing 'a degree above women.'" But it was not just the sexism of the march that disturbed them. Paula Giddings said that Farrakhan represented "nineteenth-century solutions to twenty-first century problems."[3]

In the face of so much criticism, march organizers invited three respected black women—Dorothy Height, president of the National Council of Negro Women; the poet Maya Angelou; and the civil rights pioneer Rosa Parks, known as "mother of the civil rights movement"—to be among the speakers. They also tried to play down the role of Louis Farrakhan, saying he was only one of the leaders behind the march and that he would be only one of the keynote speakers.

Ordinary African-Americans were also split in their opinions about the march. Many black men responded to the idea of showing solidarity and brotherhood, and many black women supported the march as a way for black men to feel good about themselves. Many of those who favored the march had strong misgivings about Louis Farrakhan's role in it but felt that their support of the goals of the march outweighed those misgivings.

In Camden, New Jersey, so many schoolteachers asked for the day off that classes had to be canceled. In Philadelphia, school bus service was suspended because so many drivers planned to attend the march. Sixteen hundred buses were scheduled to leave New York City beginning just after midnight the Sunday prior to the march. Amtrak had put on two additional trains. The Washington, D.C., subway system, which ordinarily did not operate from late night to early morning, would be open an additional five hours beginning at 12:30 A.M. Monday morning.

The day dawned bright and cool, the sunrise casting

a glow upon the men who had slept out on the mall overnight and upon the crowds of men who were making their way to the march meeting place. By late morning, the crowd had reached its peak. How many were there? The National Parks Service estimated 400,000. March organizers insisted that they had exceeded their goal of one million. Whatever the number, it was huge—the largest group of black people ever to have converged on Washington, D.C. They wore suits and ties, work clothes and overalls, blue jeans and hooded sweatshirts. They were young and old, Christians and Muslims, professionals and laborers and the unemployed, and of every hue of the spectrum from light to dark. Many men brought their sons to share in the historic moment. Here and there a few women could be spotted, in attendance to support black men. It was a happy crowd, a proud crowd.

Officials of the District of Columbia had feared that it might be an unruly crowd, and thus government offices had shut down. Many white politicians wished to avoid the controversy of the March, and few were available to the press that day. Many other people had stayed home from work, and many whites, except a smattering of anti-black protesters, feared to venture anywhere near the demonstration. March organizers had planned for crowd control, and the Fruit of Islam were out in force. But there was not a single incident of violence, or even unruliness the entire day.

Nevertheless, the speakers' podium was protected by bulletproof glass.

In the course of the formal program, many people stepped up to that podium. In the early part of the day,

While estimates of the number who attended the Million Man March vary, this view of the Capitol Mall, looking toward the Washington Monument, reveals a sea of humanity. In his speech, Farrakhan referred to the "sea that is before us and behind us and around us." (AP/Wide World Photos)

Chicago minister Al Sampson, a longtime supporter of Louis Farrakhan, hailed Farrakhan's leadership: "I stand here today to ask your permission to make a motion: I make a motion that we accept Minister Louis Farrakhan as our leader, all over the world, for black men, for generations yet unborn, that he be our leader, today, yesterday, and tomorrow."[4]

The Reverend Jesse Jackson, speaking in the afternoon, sounded the theme of political empowerment: "What can a million men do? Eight million unregistered black voters . . . The Gingrich forces won by nineteen thousand votes. They're cutting Medicaid; they're cutting Medicare; they're cutting scholarships; they're cutting legal assistance for women who are battered, victims of domestic violence. Well, my friends, we got the power. Victims, we got the power. [In 1960, Democrat John F.] Kennedy beat [Republican Richard] Nixon by one hundred and twelve thousand votes. What does eight million votes mean? [In 1968] Nixon beat [Democrat Hubert] Humphrey by five hundred thousand. What does eight million votes mean? We have the power, by 1996, to send Gingrich, and Gramm, and Dole back into private life. Use your vote. We have the power to change the course."[5]

The last speaker of the day was Louis Farrakhan. He spoke for more than two and a half hours, finishing only as the sun was setting. It was a wide-ranging—some called it rambling—speech in which he touched on arcane areas, such as numerology, that few understood. He blamed the press for trying to create divisiveness among black people and for trying to sabotage the march.

Farrakhan said that the people who had come to

Louis Farrakhan preaching at the Million Man March on October 16, 1995, flanked by Fruit of Islam bodyguards and standing behind a bulletproof shield. The success of the march strengthened Farrakhan's claim to a legitimate leadership role among American blacks. (AP/Wide World Photos)

Washington had answered a call from God, and that he was the messenger through whom the call had come. "Although the call was made through me, many have tried to distance the beauty of this idea from the person through whom the idea and the call was made. Some have done it mistakenly and others have done it in a malicious and vicious manner. Brothers and sisters, there is no human being through whom God brings an idea that history doesn't marry the idea with that human being no matter what defect was in that human being's character. . . . It would be silly to try to separate Moses from the Torah or Jesus from the Gospel or Muhammad from the Qu'ran. When you say, 'Farrakhan, you ain't no Moses, you ain't no Jesus, and you're not no Muhammad. You have a defect in your character,' well, that certainly may be so. However, according to the way the Bible reads, there is no prophet of God written up in the Bible that did not have a defect in his character. So today, whether you like it or not, God brought the idea *through me*, and he didn't bring it through me because my heart was dark with hatred and anti-Semitism. He didn't bring it through me because my heart was dark with hatred for white people and for the human family of the planet. If my heart were that dark, how is the message so bright, the message so clear, the response so magnificent?"[6]

In addition to the people at the march, over two million American households watched it on television—more than had watched President Clinton's State of the Union address in January or the Pope's address to the United Nations a week prior to the march. Even those most critical of Louis Farrakhan had to admit that no other black leader in the United States in 1995 could have pulled off the Million Man March, whether it had attracted a million or 400,000, or riveted the nation's attention as he had. And they admitted that the void in leadership—black and white—on race relations had been a golden opportunity for Farrakhan. Even House Speaker Newt Gingrich, who had been a target of some of the oratory at the march, said at a meeting of conservatives the following day, "The march ought to be a wake-up call for all of America. And, in a wonderful irony typical of American history, all of us owe Louis Farrakhan a thank-you for having told all of us, if the pain level is great enough for him to be a leader, then we all have a lot bigger challenge to lead."[7]

A very valid question in many people's minds was: What next? Was the march a watershed in race relations or merely a one-day celebration of black manhood that would have no lasting meaning? Would any substantive programs come out of it? Was there a way to build on the momentum generated by the march?

Within days, the beginnings of a program were being planned. In Congress, an interracial group of lawmakers called on President Clinton to appoint a national commission on race relations. For their part, organizers of the Million Man March held a press conference to announce another meeting of the African American Leadership Summit in November to plan a political and economic agenda that would build on the momentum of the march.

At that press conference, Louis Farrakhan could not resist underscoring his new place in the forefront of African-American leadership. "I know you do not know me," he said, "but I know you will get to know me. And you're going to have to live with me. To some, I am a nightmare. But to others I am a dream come true."[8]

Whether Louis Farrakhan proves to be a nightmare or a dream remains to be seen. But as long as the heritage of slavery and segregation continues to take its toll on the opportunities and hopes of a large segment of the African-American population, there will be a place for a man like Louis Farrakhan.

Notes

CHAPTER 1. Louis Farrakhan, Black Spokesman
1. "The MacNeil-Lehrer News Hour," PBS, (October 16, 1995)
2. Transcript, Barbara Walters interview with Louis Farrakhan, "20/20," (April 22, 1994), pp. 3–4.

CHAPTER 3. The Early Life of Louis Farrakhan
1. "Donahue," 1990.
2. Michael Kramer, "The Charmer," *New York* magazine (October 7, 1985), p. 16.

CHAPTER 4. The Nation of Islam
1. C. Eric Lincoln, *The Black Muslims in America*, revised edition. (Boston: Beacon Press, 1973), p. 13.
2. Ibid., p. xxv.
3. Op. cit.
4. Lincoln, pp. 25–26.

CHAPTER 6. Louis Farrakhan Joins the Nation of Islam
1. David Gallen, ed. *Malcolm As They Knew Him.* (New York: Ballantine Books, 1995), p. 82.
2. "Louis Farrakhan," *1992 Current Biography Yearbook*, p. 193.
3. Lincoln, p. 3.

CHAPTER 7. The Nation Takes Notice of the Nation
1. Malcolm X. *The Autobiography of Malcolm X*, with

the assistance of Alex Haley, revised edition (New York: Ballantine Books, 1973), p. 217.
2. Ibid., p. 241.
3. Ibid., pp. 245–246.

CHAPTER 8. The End of Malcolm X
1. Michael Friedly. *Malcolm X: The Assassination* (New York: Ballantine Books, 1992), p. 138.
2. Malcolm X, p. 299.
3. Malcolm X, p. 340.
4. Friedly, p. 186.
5. *New York Times* (February 22, 1965).
6. Eliot Fremont-Smith, review of *The Autobiography of Malcolm X, New York Times* (November 5, 1965).
7. Transcript, "20/20," (April 22, 1994), p. 4.

CHAPTER 9. The Nation Torn Apart
1. Friedly, p. 237.
2. "Islam vs. Farrakhanism," Institute of Islamic Information and Education, Chicago, IL, Brochure Series No. 19 (Internet World Wide Web site yusuf921/islam_or.htm/).
3. *1992 Current Biography Yearbook*, p. 193.
4. Lawrence H. Mamiya, "From Black Muslim to Bilalian: The Evolution of a Movement," *Journal for the Scientific Study of Religion* (1982), p. 142.

CHAPTER 10. Farrakhan and Jackson
1. Adolph Reed, Jr., "The Rise of Louis Farrakhan," *The Nation* (January 21, 1991), p. 52.
2. James Haskins, *I Am Somebody! A Biography of Jesse Jackson* (Hillside, NJ: Enslow Publishers, Inc., 1992), p. 80.
3. *1992 Current Biography Yearbook*, p. 193.
4. "Jackson's Albatross?" *Newsweek* (April 23, 1984), p. 32.
5. Op. cit.

CHAPTER 11. POWER
1. "Islam's New Entrepreneur," *Newsweek* (July 13, 1987), p. 38.
2. Kramer, p. 19.
3. Larry Rohter, "Cuomo Says Farrakhan Advocates 'Ugly' Ideas," *New York Times* (October 7, 1985), p. 4.
4. Sam Roberts, "Blacks and Jews in New York Condemn Farrakhan's Views," *New York Times* (October 4, 1985), p. 1.
5. New York *Amsterdam News* (October 3, 1985).
6. Sam Roberts, "Blacks and Jews in New York Condemn Farrakhan's Views," *New York Times* (October 4, 1985), p. 192.
7. Michael Kramer, "Loud and Clear: Farrakhan's Anti-Semitism," *New York* magazine (October 21, 1985), p. 23.
8. *Newsweek* (July 13, 1987), p. 39.

CHAPTER 12. The Two Sides of the Nation of Islam
1. Bernard Holland, "An Overture from Louis Farrakhan," *Chicago Tribune* (May 19, 1993), p. 11.
2. Ibid., p. 13.
3. *Newsweek* (June 28, 1993), p. 36.
4. Harold Brackman, *Farrakhan's Reign of Historical Error* (New York: Simon Weisenthal Center, 1992).
5. Harold Brackman, *Ministry of Lies* (New York: Simon Weisenthal Center, 1994), p. 110.
6. Transcript, "20/20," p. 3.
7. "Hate Speech Defined: The Ravings of Dr. Khalid Mohammad," *Bulletin of the Center for the Study of Popular Culture* (February 1994), p. 15.
8. *Ministry of Lies*, p. 114.
9. Ibid., p. 115.
10. Ibid., p. 117.
11. Transcript, "20/20," p. 3.

CHAPTER 13. The Assassination Controversy and an Assassination Plot
1. Transcript, "20/20," p. 4.
2. M.A. Farber, "In the Name of the Father," *Vanity Fair* (June 1995), p. 66.
3. Transcript, "20/20," p. 4.
4. Farber, p. 66.
5. Ibid., p. 62.
6. Ibid., p. 52.
7. Ibid., p. 68.
8. Ibid., p. 69.
9. Don Terry, "U.S. Agrees to End Prosecution of Farrakhan Murder Plot Case," *New York Times* (May 2, 1995), p. A12.

CHAPTER 14. Farrakhan in the Fold
1. Don Terry, "N.A.A.C.P. Shows Split As Leaders Hold Meeting," *New York Times* (June 13, 1994), p. A12.
2. Don Terry, "Blacks Say Unity Seems a Bit Closer," *New York Times* (June 15, 1994), p. A16.

CHAPTER 15. The Million Man March
1. Don Terry, "Marching to the Beat of a Million Drummers," *New York Times* Week in Review (October 15, 1995), p. 1.
2. *New York Times* (October 12, 1995), p. A18.
3. Michel Marriot, "Black Women Are Split Over All-Male March on Washington," *New York Times* (October 14, 1995), p. 8.
4. "The MacNeil-Lehrer News Hour," PBS (October 16, 1995).
5. Ibid.
6. Ibid.
7. Steven A. Holmes, "After March, Lawmakers Seek Commission on Race Relations," *New York Times* (October 18, 1995), p. B9.
8. Holmes, Ibid., p. 1.

For Further Reading

BARKER, LUCIUS J., and RONALD W. WATERS. *Jesse Jackson's 1984 Presidential Campaign: Challenge and Change in American Politics.* Champaign, IL: The University of Illinois Press, 1989.

BREITMAN, GEORGE. *The Last Year of Malcolm X: The Evolution of a Revolutionary.* New York: Merit Publishers, 1967.

FRIEDLY, MICHAEL. *Malcolm X: The Assassination.* New York: Ballantine Books, 1992.

GALLEN, DAVID, ed. *Malcolm X As They Knew Him.* New York: Ballantine Books, 1996.

HASKINS, JAMES. *I Am Somebody! A Biography of Jesse Jackson.* Hillside, NJ: Enslow Publishers, Inc., 1992.

————. *Profiles in Black Power.* New York: Doubleday & Co., Inc., 1972.

————, with Kathleen Benson. *The Sixties Reader.* New York: Viking Kestrel, 1988.

KARIM, BENJAMIN, PETER SKUTCHES, and DAVID GALLEN, eds. *Remembering Malcolm.* New York: Ballantine Books, 1996.

LINCOLN, C. ERIC. *The Black Muslims in America*, revised edition. Boston: Beacon Press, 1973.

MALCOLM X, with the assistance of Alex Haley. *The Autobiography of Malcolm X.* New York: Ballantine Books, 1973.

WORMSER, RICHARD. *American Islam: Growing Up Muslim in America.* New York: Walker and Company, 1994.

Index